DRIV

C000051497

MORE ABOUT

PSYCHOLOGY

THAN SYSTEMS

John P Brown   (Cert Ed, Cert Sp Ed, ADI)
Specialist Teacher and Disability Driving Instructor

Published by: Driving is: Publications. 6 BH21 2SR
Printed by: Think Ink (01473) 400162
ISBN 978-0-9558282-0-1

1

Foreword

Contents

Dedication

Introduction

Driving Standards

FOREWORD

Dear Reader,

I began teaching people to drive whilst I was still tutoring students with Specific Educational Needs and was disappointed to find the 'one-method-fits-all' System of instruction we were expected to use, rather than the Psychological-Learning approach which I was successfully practising as a teacher. For many people, learning to drive is the uniquely stressful experience of being in a one to one relationship, whilst having their performance critically observed in a physically dangerous environment. Under such conditions I felt it was even more important that the learner's personal needs were met, rather than them being forced to fit into an impersonal system.

For a number of years I implemented Driving Development, rather than Driving Instruction and observed how individual problems were compounded by the system advocated by the Driving Standards Agency (DSA.) Most of my clients came from having experienced failure after first attempting to learn under the set system, but they so flourished when they were taught by the methods they personally found best, that I was often asked to write down my thoughts in the form of a book.

When one woman wrote that she had been, "financially and emotionally abused by driving instructors for twenty years" and begged me to publish my thoughts in order to help others, I began to think more seriously about it. The wide ranging needs of the learners who come to me have been so great, that it has taken imposed rest following an operation, to force me to have the time to write down a few of these overflowing ideas in the hope that Learners, Instructors and the DSA will begin to look at a more effective and less financially impoverishing approach to improving safety on our roads. My second book will look at the many aspects of disability, especially covering perceptual problems and is entitled:

<u>Driving is</u> turning disability into <u>Ability.</u>

One of the official road safety slogans is <u>THINK</u> and I would like to adopt this to encourage us all to think about how we are teaching, as well as learning and to link this with my educational motto;

If he does not LEARN the way you TEACH, Can you TEACH the way he LEARNS?

John Brown. (2008)   Driving is: Publications   www.drivingincludesu.co.uk

3

CONTENTS

DEDICATED TO:

Daphne my dear wife,

who over the years has guided me in what I should say, coped with what I should not have said, painstakingly read my outpourings and attempted to correct my grammar!

As she always takes a keen interest in the people I teach, they in turn regard her as an invaluable member of our partnership. She not only listens to their problems, but also understands them. I first got to know her on one of our treks into 1960s Communist Europe, when she amazed me by her natural relationship with people and her instinctive navigational skills.

Daphne, *you have continued to navigate and guide me through all the joys and difficulties of life and I want to thank you for your unstinting support, encouragement, common sense, stability and love.*

****

ACKNOWLEDGEMENTS TO:

Angela and Cam,
for reading my initial script and for their invaluable advice.

Gina,
for helping me interpret my concepts of moving from darkness to light and from despair to hope, into the artistic design used for the cover.

Richard and Rebecca,
my son and daughter, who have always challenged my ideas and actions to make certain that I never looked at situations from only one perspective and made sure I never became complacent in the way I taught.

INTRODUCTION

People have been learning to drive for over 100 years, so you might wonder why we need an alternative approach. Surely driving is an easy process which most people manage to accomplish without too much stress. I believe that over the years some professionals have made it much too complicated and unfortunately for many learners this has led to a great deal of hardship, expense, tears, failure and dismay. If they had been taught differently, it is quite possible that many would have been perfectly capable of driving competently and safely.

We then have others who pass the test easily, but lack wider experiences and ability and are terrified of driving without their instructor accompanying them and there are also those who following the accidents they are involved in, bring distress both to themselves and to others.

This book is an attempt both to help those who are struggling to learn to drive to understand why they are struggling and also to provide for those who lack the experience and skill to become safely confident. As learning should be a partnership between the teacher and the learner, it is just as important for the learner to be aware of the issues covered in this book as it is for the instructor. It is based on my personal experiences and the experiences of my clients and whilst I have camouflaged some of the situations to prevent identification, I can assure you that all the cases I refer to are real.

In no way is this meant to be a criticism of other Approved Driving Instructors' methods, but just that I have found that some may have become entrenched and inflexible in the systems they use and therefore those perfectly valid methods may have become inappropriate for some of their clients. The purpose of this book is to look at Personalised Learning, rather than Systemised Instruction, with the client being regarded as the most important person in the learning process, the ADI becoming their adviser and the system taking on the role of an information resource.

When I was school teaching, 80% of those with Specific Needs were male and this could possibly be linked to the general teaching methods used in early schooling which favoured verbal skills. Conversely, I have found that in this type of driving instruction, 80% of my clients are female and so the majority of the examples I give are about women. This should not in any way be regarded as a negative comment on the general ability of women drivers, but that circumstances may affect them in different ways.

Many males, without Specific Needs, can succeed to pass the Test under the instructional, task orientated methods normally used. On the other hand some females may struggle under this method, but then thrive when using a personalised educational approach to their learning. This can result in them driving with increased awareness, which may be acquired as a result of greater analysis, understanding and ownership.

In no way is this book an academic study, but just a 'common sense talk'. I don't expect readers necessarily to agree with me, as my ideas have come from my own experiences, but I do hope it will encourage individuals to think and develop their own methods. I believe that 'success breeds success' and although some may see failure as a motivator, too much failure usually leads to the 'feeling of being a failure,' which can then interfere with progressive learning.

It is a study of how people Learn to Drive and therefore how to Teach People to Drive. I believe that for many people, driving is more about emotions and psychology than following a set structure which is detached from their daily experiences. Psychology is the study of how people learn and behave and I believe this should be a vital aspect of teaching people to drive.

Each chapter is written in the form of a paper which could be taken as the basis of a topic for a discussion group, or as part of a Continuous Professional Development (CPD) training session.

****

I hope you will find that I have written from the heart and have been open and honest in the issues I have raised. I want this to be an interactive experience, so please feel free to send me your own comments and personal experiences to:

systems2people@yahoo.co.uk

Further information can be obtained from:

www.drivingincludesu.co.uk
****

I trust you find this an easy read and I wish you all stimulating thoughts and happy and safe motoring.

DRIVING STANDARDS

I am sure that all those involved in teaching people to drive would say they were committed to raising driving standards, but the pass level and accident rates of our young people would indicate that we are not being successful. If it is true, that those involved are very committed, but we are still not achieving the results, then I would suggest that it is necessary to look at whether aspects of the system are defective, or whether it is in fact the system itself which may be the cause of the failure. All the dedication and effort will continue to be wasted if there is a fundamental flaw and rather than just continuing in the same vein, it will be necessary to look back to see what has happened in the past, to analyse where the problem started and so enable us to return to that point of breakdown.

If we look at the history of learning to drive, maybe we can shed light on what may be contributing to the present situation. In 1935, as the result of the very high accident rates when compared to the number of cars on the road, Government Driving Tests were introduced and initially were effective in reducing the rates of those killed and seriously injured. Anyone who deemed themselves to be a good driver was able to set themselves up as a driving instructor. The majority of examiners came from groups such as the Royal Automobile Club and the Institute of Advanced Motorists, who had proved their advanced driving ability by undertaking voluntary tests. There were also those who were retired Police and Army drivers, who had gained considerable experience from their work commitments.

In the early 1970s, it was decided to turn driving instruction into a regulated profession with the introduction of entrance tests, followed by regular Check Tests under the control of the Department of Transport. By this time we were entering a new era, where people did not only learn to drive because they wanted to drive and had the acumen, but because it became necessary to drive. Dr Beeching had closed most of the rural railway lines, cars were becoming cheaper and more reliable, people were commuting and the era of the motorway had arrived. The existing instructors were accepted into the new profession and given Grandfather Rights and under the Trainee Licence System, new instructors were given six months to enable them to practise at being driving instructors before they had to take their tests of qualification.

I think we can already see where the system was beginning to have problems. Instead of producing a new model, the existing instructors were being used to train new instructors in the historical methods they had been using for years, and the examiners were then expected to Check Test those instructors, without they themselves gaining any teaching qualifications. The difference between instruction and teaching is that, an instructor tells the person what they should be doing and it becomes an exercise in developing obedience to a set system. Hopefully, in time, this obedience can be performed instinctively with little thought or understanding necessarily being required. Teaching is helping the learner to internalise their learning and develop their personal thinking through non directed educational means. This enables them to then make their own choices and to be equipped to act rationally without an instructor. I believe that the issuing of a licence after having only received strict, but limited instruction, lies at the root of some of our young road deaths and also leads to the failure of many thinking and conscientious drivers who find they cannot flourish or pass their tests under this kind of instruction. Instruction is system based obedience, whilst teaching is people based learning.

In effect, we were thrown back to an era of examination under army and police instructional methods, without taking into account that the clientele and circumstances had changed. This was the time that the instructors and examiners should have begun to be re-trained in teaching skills, to add to their instructional skills. Instead, new instructors were given a one hour theory exam, half an hour testing of their own driving skills and half an hour's test of their instructional ability. I think the question will already be in most people's minds, 'but where was the teacher training?" How could a half hour test give any indication as to their teaching ability, especially since the examiners themselves were not teachers? As many of the examiners had also never been instructors, it would appear that the Check tests were an exercise in the examiner actually learning on the job, through observing the instructors they were testing.

In 1986, the Potential Driving Instructor (PDI) practical testing times were doubled and as at present, the trainee licences only came into force after first achieving success at both the theory and practical driving assessment levels. It will be obvious to see the pattern emerging of more of the same, but really with no valid changes being implemented; the same instruction, the same assessment, but with little relevant education being taught and certainly no consideration of the changing needs of the nation.

In 1990 the responsibility for testing moved away from the Department of Transport, to the newly created Driving Standards Agency.

Again, a golden opportunity was missed and instead of moving forward to implement a teaching approach, which would be more relevant for the millennium, they clung onto the obsolete instructional system of the past. But it did not stop there, since they sought advice about how to manage this instruction from academics and Civil Servants, who obviously demonstrated little understanding of driving or how to teach people to drive. They came up with the worst of both worlds; their system for instruction and their management of the system. Instead of focusing on the needs of Learners and Instructors and on the Psychology of how people learn, they put in place the destructive System of today where unique individuals are forced into inflexible boxes labelled 'Core Competences,' which are further sub divided into; 'fault identification,' 'fault analysis,' 'remedial action,' and 'question and answer techniques'.

The whole concept of instructors being expected to force learners into these narrow boxes has created an unsuccessful system, which has only compounded the problems that many people naturally have when learning to drive. The Driving Instruction Industry has applied this theoretical model and 'identified' the DSA faults; they have been 'analysed' and now instructors are in the position of asking pertinent 'questions'; in order for them to be equipped to take appropriate 'remedial' action. They have 'pulled up by the side of the road' and are now 'recapping' on the problems created during the journey of the past four decades.

In recent years many instructors have entered the profession from different backgrounds with their personal experiences of non-directive education and have brought a broader range of skills to the business. However, the system seems to be scared of them and unable to accommodate this new thinking breed of instructors who are questioning, not only if the imposed methods are correct, but also, the inexperience of some of the examiners who are judging them and more fundamentally, questioning the skills and experience of the policy makers themselves.

It will not benefit us by going too far back into history, but the formation of the DSA is the breakdown point to which we need to return and recognise the failure of the system from its premise, to its implementation and its daily 'chaotic' function of crisis management. As the nation has largely moved from wishing to drive, to the necessity of driving; even for those people who struggle with Specific Needs, it is essential that we formulate the teaching to suit the needs of the individual students. It is not now a selection process just to prove mechanical competence, as it was half a century ago, but the development of an essential life-skill and the system must therefore not only accommodate these candidates, but welcome them and understand their needs and the psychology of their learning.

If I asked one to describe how they learnt to walk, or play an instrument, or learnt a language, many people would admit that they would not have succeeded under a set system, because no latitude exists in a fixed system for those pupils of low ability, different ability, low self esteem or different learning styles: therefore it also cannot be an applicable system to use when teaching people to drive. Its inappropriateness is further compounded by Potential Driving Instructors being trained to instruct in this unsuitable manner. If, through their own previous experience or empathy, they turn a blind eye to a candidate's minor faults, in order to boost confidence and effectively tackle the major issues in a different way, they are likely to fail their qualifying exams; because it is not being done to the system approved by the DSA. Those who do succeed, are either perfecting a role play charade, or maybe they are even unaware of the needs of the different types of clients. A pianist may be technically perfect, but that does not make them a success. It is the X factor which is needed and by insistence on technical ability, the DSA system is rejecting many of the people we need in the business, who can think on their feet and adapt their teaching to meet the needs of the individual students.

The art of a good teacher is to be able to adapt the system and find the best way for the pupil to learn effectively, but those instructors who practise or demonstrate this skilled art, may fail their Check Test assessment, or be marked down and even if the Supervising Examiners have the experience and teaching ability to recognise these skills, they are unauthorised to step outside of the set boxes. The DSA system may work in a static classroom situation, but it manifests a lack of understanding of the extra factors involved in how people learn to drive, in what is in effect a dangerous and constantly changing environment.

With the farcical role play option, it is possible to qualify as instructors, having never taught a single learner to drive, but because they have demonstrated that they can perform a lesson to fit the set artificial system, they become 'qualified'. On the other hand excellent instructors can fail, because they were experienced at dealing with real learners and took this into account by meeting the specific needs of their pupil, outside of the set boxes. The system we have cannot truly measure teaching ability, enthusiasm, patience, determination, compassion, humour, understanding, a good teaching relationship, a reassuring smile, or the ability to encourage. These are the talents required to be a good teacher, not the ability to instruct within a constantly critical and inflexible system.

I feel sorry for the DSA staff with whom I regularly communicate, because they are good people trying their best, but they are totally overwhelmed and we, the driving instructors, have to try to cope with the resulting chaos and attempt to mediate between the DSA and our clients. It is obvious why the system is failing and yet because of vested interests, no one is prepared to say enough is enough and so we have a system which has been allowed to continue, because through its failure, it makes money. The more it fails, the more of the same poisonous medicine is given and the more ill our new drivers become. The system then tries to cover its failure by blaming the learners and their instructors and the stronger medicine then prescribed is to make the tests even harder. The pass levels fall, because of the inappropriate methods being insisted upon and so again the tests are made harder. If it were not for the resulting deaths of our young people, it would be laughable.

If I appear to be critical of the DSA, it is because this is where the rethinking needs to take place. I do not have any axe to grind with any individual member of the DSA, since they are out of their depth and are not able to provide the goods or the services for which we are paying them. It is not their fault, but we now need someone with the guts and skills to see what is happening and listen to the concerns of parents, driving instructors and learners, to make really effective changes, rather than just implementing more of the same and so compounding the problems even further. I am not in any way anti-system, as a framework is essential for many learners, but it must be recognised as being successful and effective and flexible enough to meet the individual needs of each learner.

****

The present system cannot and will not work and the DSA, which clearly recognises this, desperately continues to try to cover this failure by implementing more of the same methods, but all this has done is lead to increased failure. Our children are worth more than what they are receiving and I hope that for some, this book is the beginning of them looking in a different direction. After nearly four decades of trying to get it right, it is now time to immediately erect a STOP sign and insist on a U turn back to 1990, to enable us all to think again.

Section 1 Personal Experiences

i) Personal Influences.

ii) Principles v Principals.

iii) Professional History.

iv) Personal Inspiration.

v) Empathy.

i)   PERSONAL INFLUENCES

The theme of these books is to look at how early influences can have an effect on one's behaviour and learning and how an analysis of these experiences can sometimes help one to cope with the present. At first I thought it inappropriate to write about myself, but realised that maybe reference to my own experiences and an understanding of them, would help readers to also appreciate where I am coming from. I therefore apologise for my personal indulgences, but hope some readers will find them interesting and understand the reason for them being included in a book about teaching and learning and maybe help them to analyse why their own background could be causing them to find aspects of learning to drive more problematic than they had expected.

I was born in Manchester into a deeply religious Protestant family providing strict Church of England boundaries. My father had a strong sense of right and wrong, loyalty, tradition, beliefs and education and to be really accepted I was expected to remain within those boundaries. Within these accepted rules, my mother was a free-thinker, who had an enquiring mind and loved discussing with her many friends. Discussion was a part of family life and you never 'lost an argument', it was just a difference of opinion, but however heated it became it never led to any animosity. As my parents were representatives of a pioneer missionary society, we had numerous visitors from all over the world, who helped to enrich my knowledge and experiences and taught me think in a broader way. My father left school at the age of thirteen and worked at the Cooperative Society for fifty years until he retired. We did not have a television or radio and received most of our social insight through reading the Manchester Guardian and although we were not politically liberal/socialists, we had an acute awareness of poverty and the plight of the disadvantaged and so the care of others was uppermost in our view of life. Income was a key factor, as we were quite poor and money had to be spent carefully and ethically. We learnt to make-do and mend. Waste was a sin, so there was no alcohol or cigarettes or anything frivolous, but it still remained a happy and stimulating home.

My maternal grandfather had been a strict Edwardian father, but also a free-thinker, traveller and Methodist. Fortunately I was the youngest grandchild and he had mellowed somewhat by the time I knew him. Nothing was boring or beneath him and there were no obstacles which could not be overcome. He fostered my great interest in life and I can see him now with his headphones listening to the schools' programmes on radio which enabled him to continue learning, even though in his eighties his eyesight was failing him. He had been a professional artist, mostly dealing with lithographic advertising for Robertson's Jams, the Cotton Industry and the promotion of holidays at Southport and on the Lancashire coast.

Practical ability came easy to me and academia was something I would have welcomed but, partly owing to my home location just over the border in Lancashire, the opportunity of a grammar school education was not one I could attain until the age of seventeen, after attending various other schools. I think I succeeded better by being towards the top of a lower group, than at the bottom of a higher group, but I am acutely aware of the gaps in my education. My varied schooling helped me relate to a wide cross section of people from many different academic and social levels. I learnt by watching and asking questions and my real joy was to sit in the local railway signal box, or watch the road menders and builders at work.

I trained as a teacher at Matlock Teachers' Training College, but because they had no vacancies on the Secondary Geography course and they did not offer Economics or Politics, I studied Primary and Divinity. I can remember very few things which really fired my imagination, but I enjoyed the teaching practices and it gave me the chance to grow and develop my own interests in both driving and travel. I do remember one art activity session when the lecturer had us looking at the fluff in the corner of the room. The message was a foundation laying one for me. Don't only look for the obvious, look at everything from a different angle. If you only look at the room, you will only see the room, but if you look deeper, you will be fascinated by what you see. Our drama lecturer gave us an exercise, where we all had to emphasise our given word in a sentence in a variety of ways so as to make a completely different meaning. I found that a seven word sentence could have seven different meanings. Again it taught me the value of communication and how to view from another angle, rather than judging just from my own perspective or understanding.

I cashed my National Savings Certificates to pay for driving lessons and further developed my skills by driving the women's sports teams in the college's old crash gearbox Morris Commercial and 'new' Commer minibus. It was still a time when women did not see driving as a priority and it was mostly left to the males. I obtained my PSV double-decker bus licence in Nottingham and in 1964 we took a group of students on a double-decker expedition to Moscow in a Leyland PD1 and the following year I drove an AEC Burlingham coach to Kiev. This was the beginning of numerous expeditions for me behind the iron curtain, which culminated in a fascinating visit to Albania when it was still a closed land. On a few occasions I have been likened to Michael Palin and once, a lady in New Zealand thanked me for my travel programmes and assured me that she avidly watched all of them! How I wished I had been fortunate enough to make all those fascinating journeys. I retained my bus licence by driving at weekends for Mayne's Coaches of Clayton, mainly taking supporters to the Manchester City and Manchester United matches and in the summertime drove visitors on day trips to the seaside or zoo.

****

Throughout my time as a driving instructor I have observed that a major factor affecting how people learn, or how successful a learner will be, can often be traced back to previous life influences. These can deeply affect how free people are to both act and react appropriately and how effectively they can assimilate new information. Experiences which have been deeply suppressed into the subconscious can under stress be resurrected and seriously affect the ability to learn. Whilst these flashbacks may have a negative influence, other positive experiences can be built on to create a successful learning environment. It depends on the skill of the instructor who can either foster or hinder this development.

ii) PRINCIPLES v PRINCIPALS

"The headmaster wants you to report to his office after school". The order came when I was in my first teaching job in a Lancashire Primary school. My class consisted of forty five 7-8 year olds, who were contained all day in a small prefabricated room. We did not have a hall or any other covered facilities, although we did have an outside playground for break times which we could use if it was timetable for us and it was not raining. I was employed, not only to teach every academic subject, but also PE, Art, Music, Drama and to give the pupils a sound grounding in Reading and Spelling. My teacher training had left me quite unprepared to cope for such a situation, so I had to rely on my instincts, ingenuity and personal skills to provide these children with a reasonably broad education.

I knocked on the headmaster's door and upon hearing the call "enter", walked into the office and fought my way through the fog to where the headmaster had been sitting all day chain smoking. I stood in trepidation in front of him as he stated, "I have observed that you have introduced unauthorised reading material into your teaching programme. 'Look and Say' is the way we teach reading and 'Janet and John' is the best reading scheme ever published, so you will only use that system." I had the temerity to ask what I should use to teach the pupils who were failing under the Janet and John Scheme and summoned the courage to also ask what I should say to the parents who questioned me about the progress of their children. A stony stare: a deep drag on yet another cigarette and the response which was the defining moment in my educational philosophy. "Adjust their reading ages, so the parents will believe their children are making progress."

He continued to explain, that he was certain it was only a matter of maturation preventing children from reading and when the children reached the age to be able to read, they would do so under the Janet and John Scheme, since it was the "best scheme in the world." Apparently, he believed, the pupils would then catch up with the rest of the class. "Just add a few months to their reading age, because my pupils will learn by the Look and Say method," he stated emphatically.

My six years at that school gave me a thorough grounding in how children learn and it taught me that I had to find my own way around problems, to find solutions which met the needs of the students, without upsetting the system. I arrived at my own totally unscientific and personal estimations that 25% of children would succeed irrespective of the teacher, methods or situation; that 50% could be taught in a standard way and that 25% needed detailed analysis of their needs and to be introduced to the specific kind of teaching they required. I learnt to be suspicious of educational fads, rules, political systems and statistics and people who, because of their position, thought it was their right to dictate to others how they should learn and what they should think. I also accepted that the majority of people found those systems and boundaries comforting and correct for them since they provided them with the security they needed.

It made sense to me, that some children had auditory strengths, some had visual strengths and some had semantic strengths. If I only provided one way, as I was expected to, then I was obviously depriving the others of the education they required. What I wanted to do was to provide the child with the material which suited their needs the best. I therefore wrote my own phonic worksheets to supplement the 'Look and Say' approach stipulated by the school and made story cards to stimulate the children's practical interests and fantasies.

One example of coping within the stipulated 'system' in the classroom, whilst also meeting the needs of my pupils, was that I moved away from the traditional pristine nature table, and provided an exploration or junk corner which was full of electric motors, telephones, car batteries, clocks, electrolysis experiments, packaging, nature observations, worms, wood, saws, screws, etc. (probably none of this would be allowed today in case the little darlings learnt by hurting themselves.) The work cards I wrote met the needs of some of the children who were failing under the reading scheme and some parents saw me in the street and thanked me for what I had done to make their offspring, usually sons, take an interest in education and realise that learning can be exciting. The headmaster seemed placated as the reading material I introduced was not in conflict with his preferred reading scheme, since the children "chose" to read them for interest and they were not being read in reading lessons.

I believe we are taking away the fun of success from driving, just as strict adherence to one system did with reading. Driving should be fun. Are we making life too difficult for our new drivers and creating problems they do not need to have?

Upon leaving the school, the ditty written for me by the deputy head, who had a better understanding of the wider aspects of education and teaching, focused on my notoriously chaotic junk table. It was of little interest to many of my class, as they did not need it, but I saw it as a major teaching aid for the 25% of pupils whom I believed needed a different approach. It gave them a joy of learning and an understanding of the reasons for education and they discovered that learning should and could be fun.

Often the child who is having problems and 'creating' a nuisance is the one who could be a great success, because he is the most 'creative.' There are many ways to skin a rabbit, as my grandmother would have said and the teacher's job is to find the one which is best for the individual student and not to follow a set formula. My deputy head's poem summed up what others saw, but the students who needed a different way saw it as the key to their learning, since it provided them with an interest in education and a wider experience of how they could gain knowledge.

Bishop ***, Comprehensive, High,
Have no fear, John Brown is nigh.
On M*** Road he's turned his back,
Sad? Sorry? Not our Jack.
If you've a fuse to mend
A bus to drive, or money to lend
John Brown's your man.
But, let your shelves and cupboards beware-
Pins and needles, pots and pans,
Batteries, wheels, tins and cans,
Paper models, rails and rods,
Bits and pieces, odds and sods,
All are grist to John Brown's mill.
Therefore, teachers, pupils too,
Wear your glasses,
Ere you trip upon your as---.

I therefore determined to spend my career looking at the needs of the 25% of students whom I believed required a special approach to their learning and consequently their teaching. Hence my different approach to the teaching of driving and those who have problems. I became a pragmatist, not a purist and came to believe in exercising common sense, rather than implementing an inflexible system. In no way am I suggesting that the received methods used by other instructors are wrong, but just that they may not be appropriate to the specific needs of certain candidates; nor am I suggesting that many instructors do not use the same techniques as I use, but they have probably come to the work from a different direction and may not explain the reasons for their methods from the same roots. Just like my headmaster, some people will regard my comments as heretical, frightening or even dangerous, but at least I hope I stimulate thought and discussion and a reappraisal of the thinking about set driving schemes which are blindly accepted by some, as the only truth.

Does it really matter if you don't dot your 'i' or cross your 't' in the prescribed order, as long as the results are achieved?

Whilst teaching children to read, I realised that it was important not to lose sight of the fact that I was teaching children - not reading; and so with teaching people to drive, I am teaching people- not driving. Many readers will be able identify the various reading fads as their own stumbling blocks on their path towards fluent reading; Phonics, ITA, Look and Say, Real Books; these have all been responsible for destroying the learning for some students, whilst others have flourished under these exclusive systems. What we required was an analysis of the needs of the child and a balanced approach to their teaching and the same holds true with driving. We need an analysis as to the most appropriate methods to use, before we begin the lessons and that should be based on the skill of the instructor and therefore where the root of instructor training should lie.

During my study of teaching dyslexics, Dr Harry Chasty, our Psychology Lecturer, posed the question; **"If he does not learn the way you teach, can you teach the way he learns?"** I adopted this as my educational motto and have used it ever since, as it applies as much to teaching driving as it does to teaching reading. Ask someone what is the most important skill they learnt as a child and most will reply "to read," then ask the most important skill as an adult; most will say "to drive." Both skills provide freedom, social, career and educational opportunities, fun and independence; but sadly some people are prevented from attaining these goals, by inappropriate instruction and methods.

****

It is now recognized that the teaching towards and the testing required for the National Curriculum, has so over stressed many of our school children, that it has contributed to them becoming some of the most unhappy children in the developed world and a large number are still failing to succeed to read. I would think there is a strong correlation between the stress of pressurised learning and this resulting failure and so it has become a self fulfilling prophecy. I believe we can draw a close parallel, between what has happened in our schools and compare this with the increasing difficulties of the driving tests and some of the inappropriate methods used for teaching driving. Together these have probably contributed to producing many of the stressed learners we see on our streets, who when they eventually do pass their tests, may still be ill equipped for everyday driving. This in turn adds to our statistically poor road safety record and the KSI (Killed and Seriously Injured) tragedies of some of our young people on today's roads.

iii) PROFESSIONAL HISTORY

In some ways Primary-age children were not my forte, but the experience gained by teaching these seven and eight year olds gave me an insight into how people learnt and I became fascinated by those who found school difficult. From parental feedback, I knew that I was relating more easily to those children, than to the more able students whom I found to be quite boring. Many of those seemed to need to be spoon fed who just performed the tasks which were set and appeared to me to lack that individual spark which made them different.

I remember one of my 'differently-challenged' boys who wrote a very interesting story, but it was so totally mirrored, that I could only read it when I actually looked at it in a mirror. I had never come across this before and tactfully suggested he copied it out again, so that I could display it on the wall; (or shall I say the ceiling, as it was a prefab with no wall space). He rewrote it and without knowing, transcribed it back into perfectly written English. I do so wish I had kept this example, as I have never come across any other mirror writing as perfect as his was. I wondered how his mind actually worked and would now be quite interested to know if he had experienced any problems when learning to drive. I also remember a girl who wrote copiously perfectly scripted pages, consisting of o, a, e, and s and submitted them for her story work, but they related to nothing that I was able to decipher. She was just performing in the way she thought was required, but without any understanding.

I wonder how many learn to drive by rote, but without real understanding!

After six years, I took up a post as Head of Remedial Department in an Inner City Secondary School, but with coming from a different background I was able to see where the education was failing and was given a free hand to revolutionise the teaching of those 'differently-abled' students by changing the emphasis from teacher-based instruction, to student-based learning. I found that even at Secondary Level, some were still failing to read the same books which they had struggled to read when in Primary School. It seemed obvious that if they were not succeeding, then we had to approach the problem from a variety of totally different directions, until we found an appropriate solution.

My starting question was, "What are the students interested in?" For most of the boys this was driving, so on the usual 'wag day' of Friday I timetabled all the wider aspects of driving. To me it seemed much more sensible to teach reading from a workshop manual, than by reading about Janet and John going to primary school with Mummy and Daddy and of course, it was more successful. I hope I made education more relevant to some but as it was trial and error, I am acutely aware of my failures and experimentation. My real educational teaching began when I was seconded on a course to look at Specific Needs Provision in the Ordinary School and went to Manchester College of Education. Here at last, I met teachers who understood how I thought and felt about education and learning. I had found my niche.

The school leaving age was raised to sixteen and I was put in charge of the ROSLA students, (Raising Of School Leaving Age) who resented having to stay on at school for an extra year and I was responsible for devising courses for these non academic students. I prepared examination studies which I felt were more relevant to disaffected students, such as "Preparation for Driving," which involved the theory of driving, practical maintenance, road development, the environment, recycling, map reading, design, automotive industry, the science of road safety, the fuel industry, commerce and transportation, mathematics and world economics, statistics and green issues etc. It was a vast subject and encompassed everything that any curriculum could have wished for.

Those who wanted to develop their ideas were encouraged to do so, whilst those who felt safer undergoing set work, were also able to succeed at their own level of achievement. There is nothing new under the sun and it amuses me to hear of all these 'new' initiatives for Road Safety, which we were successfully tackling in schools in the 1970s. The professional teachers then had the freedom to help the students achieve their own individual successes, at different, but more suitable levels. These students left school with relevant educational knowledge, some qualifications and a practical skill. Those who could not cope with all the academic knowledge, which they knew they did not want and knew they would never require, did not become failures because we developed their strengths and interests, instead of undermining them by unproductive study.

It is so sad to see the present regressive policies, where Learners fail to drive because of their struggle with the complexities of the Theory Test. They may just want to cut the grass and be groundsmen or builders, but now, everything has to be academically based, instead of founded on skill and practical understanding. This discriminates against the huge numbers of people, who are not and never will be academic and contributes towards turning them into failures and misfits in our Society, which in turn, then has to try to pick up the pieces. It is such a short sighted and backward policy, that it must be changed as soon as possible. There were many progressive ideas and policies in the seventies and yet with all the money spent since then, the reading levels have not improved and the students feel they are now greater failures because of the over emphasis on these academic qualifications, instead of them just being accepted as good and valuable members of society.

The reason for this failure seems quite clear, in that our taxes used for reading development were spent on politically influenced policies and it would appear as if the same is now happening with driving. This time it is the client's money which is being wasted on inappropriate lessons and unacceptable academic tests, ostensibly to force a reduction in the level of car usage; but the most affected clients are those in rural areas, who need to drive because of the lack of a rural transport system. If there was any indication of it being a successful policy to reduce the KSI amongst our young drivers, then there may be some justification, but instead the opposite would appear to be true.

After leaving Manchester I spent many years working within the Special Needs Department for Dorset Educational Support Service, teaching children whose Specific Needs were not being met within the ordinary school and later on those who were 'Statemented' under the 1981 Education Act, or those who were, 'not accessing the curriculum at the level of their intellectual ability.' I must make a clear distinction here between Special Educational Needs and Specific Educational Needs. The latter is a subsection of Special Education and involves students of average or above average ability, who have a specific problem, or problems which hinder their ability to succeed at the level which one might expect. I have taught students whose writing, to the untrained eye, is unreadable and spelling indecipherable, but who with specific help have progressed to get good degrees. In the past, they may have been regarded as almost ineducable, because we were actually testing the wrong things.

We again seem to be increasingly testing inappropriate things in the Driving Tests and producing failures out of promising students.

Numerous courses and experiences later, I decided in 1990 to merge together my two passions of driving and education and to train myself as an Approved Driving Instructor, but as I did not wish to teach 'normal' clients, or to instruct in the DSA way, I largely taught myself. I was already a member of The Institute of Advanced Motorists and so bought in a few sessions with a retired examiner to advise me as to what the DSA required. As often happens in life, plans changed and I was offered a post tutoring Dyslexic, Dyspraxic, ASD, ADHD and overseas students in a residential private school and so had a captive 6th form of students who wanted to learn to drive before they entered university. What I discovered was, that some of the students who had problems with their academic work, also had problems with their driving and I began to study the correlation between Specific Needs and Driving Difficulties and the rest is written in these books.

When I realised that little was being done for these students who wanted to drive and in fact some were being disadvantaged by the way they were being instructed, I left school teaching to specialise in providing for their needs and to try to educate others that some learners may require a different way of teaching. The more my work became known, the more referrals came in from diverse agencies, from Education and Social Services, to the Medical Profession. The main medical referrals came following head injuries, illness and ageing problems.

****

I have learnt a huge amount about education from driving instruction, but believe that without my specialist educational background, I would have found it difficult to succeed with the complexity of the problems with which I have been presented. Together with the student, we have been able to analyse their individual problems, which would not usually be possible in class teaching situations and so they have not only achieved success at driving, but also incidentally, have increased their own self esteem and furthered their personal development.

iv) PERSONAL INSPIRATION

Many people who enter a specialist area of care-work have had someone in their lives who has been their inspiration. Mine was my cousin Derek. Although his disabilities were extreme, dealing with him has helped me to understand many of the problems I have encountered as a driving instructor and to recognise that we need to see beyond our client's disabilities and seek out their abilities.

He was ten years my senior and born with Spina Bifida, but it was not this disability that caused his problems, but rather the associated Hydrocephalus. As a result of the un-drained fluid on the brain, he had a misshapen head, a thin skull, was obviously brain damaged and therefore classed as "backward." After leaving Special School, he managed for a while to hold down a warehouse job, which my father got for him at the Co-op and in spite of what would today be described as 'bullying in the workplace', he was quite resilient, until in his early twenties he had a catastrophic infection which totally destroyed his eyesight and all but 5% of his hearing. Even with a very powerful hearing aid, when in the street or with other extraneous noises, he was totally deaf. He was unable to learn Braille, or how to use a stick to guide himself, but owing to the brain damage, his major disabilities were his anxiety and his inability to reason.

On the other hand, when he became relaxed, we found he had a brilliant memory and areas of his brain unaffected by his disability showed quite a high level of intelligence. His attitude was extremely positive and he was game for any adventure my wife or I could devise for him. Most people could only see the disabilities, but by being in close contact, we learnt to see his abilities and found that even though he did have many specific disabilities, if we had viewed these as a general disability, then we would have been unable to appreciate all his strengths, feelings and desires. It would not only have become discriminatory on our part, but we would have missed out on many corporate joys and experiences.

In one traumatic week, both our mothers, who were sisters, died of cancer. As I lived in Dorset and Derek lived in Manchester, he was taken into Local Authority Care, but what care do you provide for someone who is Deaf-Blind, of low intelligence, who had just been bereaved and had no one to advocate for him? The imposed solution was, most inappropriately, an Old Peoples' Home for the Blind. Little understanding or provision was made for his deafness and yet this was his primary disability. How do you cope without communication? Fortunately he had memories and could speak, so when we visited he expressed his total frustration at his predicament, especially as he was still a relatively young man and to cut a long story short, he asked to be trained in independent living to enable him to look after himself in his own flat. We became his advocates and supporters and for 25 years he learnt to live successfully in his own flat and with daily support he cared for himself. Three times a year we took him away on holiday and provided him with many experiences and therefore he had an incredible memory bank of these adventures.

Most people asked why we did it and what benefit was it for someone who was deaf-blind to travel. When tempers got fraught, we sometimes asked ourselves why we did it and the answer was always clear; because he was enthusiastic to try everything possible; interested in everything and essentially a happy person. He loved history, music, sport and travel and swam in the Pacific breakers with a rope tied round his waist, he rode horses, he water skied, he laughed at every ridiculously amusing situation, he played bowls, he rode tandems, he threw balls at the coconut shy, he listened to the radio and in the quietness he would talk at length about the programmes he had heard, especially about his beloved Lancashire Cricket and Manchester United.

His laugh was infectious and many a time his fun was catching and a restaurant would echo with laughter as he tried to eat Pizza with Mozzarella cheese. People warmed to him and he was our entrance ticket to many experiences, because he was so enthusiastic and interested. We took him on buses, boats, trains, planes and travelled many thousands of miles by car through America, Hawaii, Britain and Europe. Whenever we stopped, I would describe to him what was happening and what we were seeing. I took him round museums and art galleries and can remember the laughter as he felt nude statues and then gradually realised what they were. I can remember the crowds who used to gather and follow us round as I loudly communicated to him what I was seeing and the visitors presumed I was the local guide. I wonder what misconceptions the tourists went away with as I made up the stories to make it more realistic. Years later he would proclaim "John do you remember when we saw?" He saw through my eyes, but those images reached his soul and his memory became mine, as he remembered things I had been able to see with my eyes, but which had long been forgotten; crowded out by life's hustle and bustle.

The down sides to caring for him were numerous, but we could always just look at what he overcame to return us to a thankful frame of mind. Owing to the specific area of brain damage it was not always what we could see which troubled him, but his hidden anxiety, which was at times overwhelming and difficult to cope with, since his reasoning was non existent. I remember once tactfully suggesting that the next time he came on holiday, he should bring more than a couple of pairs of underpants, so great embarrassment and anxiety resulted and the next time he arrived with forty pairs. Once when we visited, his fridge contained forty six rolls and twenty six bottles of milk. You see the home-helps had to do what the client asked, so if he asked for a bottle of milk and a packet of rolls, that is what they had to get. No question, no reason. The system came first. They were not allowed to use their common sense. One helper was reprimanded for brightening up his day by dancing with him instead of cleaning. One dealt with his care, the other tried to deal with his needs, but only care was statutory and not needs. The two requirements did not seem to be able to cross over.

After this episode we paid privately for an excellent free lance social worker to provide what he required, rather than what he in his blind ignorance asked for. His enjoyment of eating was dramatically changed as he was taken to Morrison's Supermarket and given a choice of what he bought. Derek loved beetroot on his sandwiches and his carer used to comment that when he visited, the beetroot on the walls looked as if 'murder had been committed.' A new LA Social Worker also made his daily life much better.

Sadly, as he was preparing for another holiday with us in Canada, he fell and cracked his skull. The lack of appropriate medical care was a disgrace and he contracted MRSA and 6 months later died of Meningitis. They had no provision in hospital for multiple sensory-loss handicaps and they had no idea how to deal with him and took away his hearing aid so they then did not have to try to talk to him. The problems with rigid Data Protection rules made life for us very difficult, when trying to communicate with the authorities 250 miles away. Even when we visited, discussion was very restricted, mainly because the staff did not know what to do and were embarrassed and on the defensive. He did not deserve to suffer in the way he did, but the system did not cater for people who are different.

But what am I left with? This gaunt, misshapen, deaf, blind, backward man who had such anxieties and could be so unreasonable, but who attracted such admiration and brought joy to so many people that he will always be remembered by everyone who met him. Caring for Derek has helped me enormously in my understanding of the many physically and emotionally broken drivers I have taught, who on the surface would appear to be incapable of achieving success, but beneath that exterior lay the ability and determination to succeed, if only they could be provided with the opportunities which enabled them to flourish. The primary question should be, if we made the provision, would it be possible for them to learn to drive? Start the questioning from the positive rather than the negative and it is amazing what people can achieve.

****

With having advocated for my students with Education Departments and for Derek with Local Authority and Medical Agencies over many years, it made me even more determined to fight for the rights of those whose needs were not being met by the DSA, just because they did not fit easily within the prescribed boxes. Sometimes the DSA officials may feel I am a little belligerent in my dealings with them regarding the need to modify these boxes in order to make the correct provision for those with Specific Needs: I then just think of Derek and see my work as a continuation of what I did for him. I know there are many issues which still need addressing under disability discrimination and I hope that every battle I win for those with driving difficulties is a development of his indomitable spirit and that Derek's will to succeed and enjoy life will continue to live on into future generations, by the example he set me.

v) **EMPATHY**

Empathy is the ability to enter into another's experiences and to sympathetically understand their thoughts and feelings. This desire to help others is often stimulated by situations people have encountered in their own lives. They may have struggled with a problem and failed, or overcome it, or found a way around it, or most probably a mixture of all three. People who have struggled to learn to drive often want to become driving instructors because they know that they 'understand' the problems associated with learning.

I would have preferred some of those I have taught to drive to be able to contribute to this section, (maybe that will be another book) but people usually cope with their difficulties by suppressing the way they feel, so as soon as they are successful they find the journey they have taken too difficult to analyse and write about. They therefore choose to move on and forget the pain. Learning to drive is often compared to childbirth. It is traumatic, but as soon as it is over, the pain is forgotten and it was all worth it in the end. I am therefore going to analyse my own problems in the hope that this will encourage readers to look at and discuss their personal difficulties, or for instructors to try to understand the problems of others more fully. Once we understand, we can begin to accept and come through the other side and so become better people and better teachers. Some readers will already be wondering what I am writing about, whilst others will be saying, 'that is just like me; I did not know anyone else felt the same. I thought I was the only one who felt like that'.

Although I would not really classify myself as dyslexic, I have many dyslexic tendencies, although in my school days people did not use the term and sufferers just got shouted at for being lazy, untidy, not concentrating or messing around. I am essentially dominantly right handed, but have no comprehension about how anyone can bat or golf right handed. It may be the norm, but to me it is totally impossible. Today, terms like Dyslexia, Dyspraxia, Tourettes, Aspergers and Attention Deficit Hyperactive Disorder have helped sufferers to realise that, just because they do something differently, they are not stupid or on their own and this has led to a greater understanding of the associated problems encountered by many otherwise bright and capable students.

I did not enjoy team games such as football, or anything requiring rhythm or memory sequences, although I did need rules to try to support my poor memory. Basically I just wanted to do, discover and problem solve. When assembling flat-packs or machinery I do not consult the plans; unless I am in total desperation and my wife insists; because I do not think sequentially, but when I dismantle something, I do need to draw a diagram of what I have done, otherwise I will have totally forgotten what goes where. My office, garage and bedroom have always been very untidy, because dyslexic minds flit from one thing to another and act on what they see and work things out, rather than plan or remember what they are looking for. I often cannot remember what I am seeking, so I go into a room, because that is where I know I will find what I need, but until I see it, I do not know what it is I have gone for. This can present problems, if someone decides to 'tidy up' and disturb my 'chaotic' security!

In order to help students with similar difficulties, I have marked relevant switches on the car with Tippex, and also to denote the bonnet catch lever and have labelled the 'Tell Me Show Me' service points. It is quite disconcerting if, at the beginning of the test, the candidate finds they cannot remember where the bonnet release lever is located and this memory loss can so disorientate their confidence that they can feel a failure before they have even begun the driving.

I have always had a memory recall problem which, like most sufferers, I have found acutely embarrassing and at times it has hindered me in my social and professional development. The biggest stress is that it can be unbelievably frustrating and unless I have hooks to hang my thoughts onto, to enable me to compose a whole picture, I am usually lost. I try to draw bits of information together to make a whole sense, but it does not always work correctly and sometimes the wrong conclusions can be drawn. I used 'Cloze Procedures' to complete the jigsaw to make sense of pieces of information, before I had even heard of the term. It was my own subconscious survival strategy.

When I had to remember anything, I used what I now know to be 'mnemonics,' or memory aids, to hang my thoughts onto and help me to remember. Although my visual memory was reasonable, it also helped me to use 'phonics' to learn to read, because rules were provided which I could apply to assist my spelling. Irregular spellings were and still are a great problem and my handwriting is illegible, even to me. This is not the place to discuss strategies, as there are many books available, but just to hint at a few problems that those learning to drive may have which can affect their procedural thinking and how they learn to drive.

I could always argue about the facts, because that was a flowing story, but I was no good at recalling the actual facts and if other ideas came into my mind, the facts were overwhelmed and I could not bring them to the fore. Examination revision was no good for me, so one method I used was to write down dates and formulas and constantly go over them on the morning of the examination until the doors opened. I kept repeating them in my head and as soon as we were told to "Start!" I wrote down everything I had in my mind before reading the set questions. I was then free to answer the questions, knowing that I had the facts written down to which I could then refer, if required. If I had read the questions first, they would have filled my mind and suppressed all the 'stored' facts.

I could never remember names or recall them, even when relating to people I knew very well. As a young child I was expected to touch my cap and say "Good morning Mrs. Walton" to my neighbour whenever I met her, but of course I could never recall her name, so I 'rudely' just said, "Good Morning." The correct system was impossible for me to follow, so I now rarely address people, because if I try, I am likely to get their name wrong or even worse, worry that I have got it wrong. I am sure that for this reason I am often misjudged and thought of as being rude. I can remember something obscure about the person in question, which may not be diplomatic to mention and I will be able to describe their characteristics, but I cannot recall their names or even their faces. It is quite possible that within the next few minutes, the correct response may enter my head at a most inopportune moment.

I do wonder if our perception of our learners is actually correct when they do something 'wrong,' or we do not understand, or is it actually a learnt strategy of theirs to avoid something worse? Instructors often describe the problems that their learners may be encountering and to me the reasons may seem to be quite different to what the instructor is attributing to the problem. I was recently reading an instructor's outpourings re a young woman's driving, but none of the things she was doing seemed of any real consequence, because of one question in my mind; epilepsy? Are we instructors searching hard enough for the reasons, or just seeing the manifestations?

As I wrote the previous paragraph, I used my coping strategy of leaving a blank for the name, but I find it interesting, that my neighbour's name of all those years ago, has just flitted into my head and I have been able to go back and supply it, just as I would have done in my school examinations.

Of course, I am now doubting that the name given, actually relates to the neighbour to which I am referring. Oh well, just one of the many frustrations I have always had to live with! Many of our learners have similar problems and because we cannot see into their heads, we often do not understand them. I had one lady try to open the door as we drove along and I could have screamed and shouted at her. She then explained that she knew the wiper switch was on the right, she had just chosen the wrong lever; she was not being reckless or stupid, but her mind-processing had just not got it completely right. When she explained, it was easy to understand, but I had to allow her to explain and also make her comfortable enough to be free to explain.

When I was a class teacher, I developed my strategy of preparing a student desk plan to which I could refer so as to be able to address the students appropriately. If they were not sitting in a specific place I would wander over, pick up their exercise book; ostensibly to get a better look and then refer to the name on the front so as to be able to address them appropriately. How often we search for our glasses as a cover to give us time to think or mask our fear of reading!

As a peripatetic teacher, I organised a colour-coded filing system to enable me to quickly check the names of the staff and students in the school I was visiting so that I could address them correctly. It was not easy, but I managed to cope, with only the occasional embarrassment and if I am giving a talk I need to write everything down, so that I have it there to which I can refer. In actual fact, I probably do not require it, but it is my security and I think I may need it. I try to write my notes similar to how I talk so that it does not appear as if I am reading, but I like to have a lectern on which I can rest my notes, otherwise I fear I may lose my train of thought and the freedom and professionalism I feel I would like to have. These are some of my specific strategies, but many times instructors have to realize that the learner's unusual actions may be their coping strategies, or that they may need to write something down, or practically perform something before it registers.

Even though I have learnt to cope I often cannot recall the names of my clients who may be sitting next to me, so I have to have my diary at hand to which I can refer and sometimes I muddle my words in general conversation. The substituted word may be the same length and probably begin with the same letter, but the word I utter will be incorrect and sometimes the opposite of what I want comes out, or maybe it will be an associated word.

When I 'hear' what I have actually said, I will immediately realise that it is wrong and the correct word will then come to mind, followed by a hasty correction. Fortunately it rarely ever happens with the driving instructions I give, since those are firmly established in a different part of my brain and are used regularly, although I do know I cannot work too long and get tired or the words may become muddled.

I can remember teaching one of my dyslexic students trying to form patterns of 'ight' words. We had listed 'sight, bright, light, fight, might, fright' and then I gave him the word 'night'. Excitedly he exclaimed "I can spell this word," and promptly wrote down 'dark'. Many people give associated words, instead of the correct words and may also perform associated actions, instead of the correct ones.

I was attending a course at Reading University on 'Reading and Language Skills' and was having a lecture on Hearing Loss. The lecturer picked me out from those in the study group and said "John, you have a hearing loss." I was amazed, as I did not know that I did. He added that he knew, because he had observed that I always looked at people's lips, rather than their eyes. I did not know that I lip-read because it had been something I developed over my whole life and it was just an additional unconscious support. In fact I thought everyone looked at people's lips and not their eyes. We then went into the hearing laboratory and he proved his point. I did not know that I did not hear the same as everyone else, although I knew I did not like large groups or parties and could only 'hear,' if someone was sitting opposite me.

I will not use a mobile phone because I cannot hear through any extraneous noise and hate using the telephone unless I make the phone call and have prepared what I want to say and have pen and paper available so I can make notes. I have to prepare for the conversation and it used to cause great mirth within my family when I would write down my address, my wife and children's names, the number and make of the car etc. before making a phone call, just in case I could not immediately recall them when I was asked. We have all developed our own 'stupid' supports, which enable us to cope with life and we as driving instructors need to be aware of the supports our clients desperately hold onto, in the terrifying situations we present to them.

My mind often feels it is about to crash through containing too much information but there is constant input, because everything in life is interesting and I do not want to miss anything. I must be a nightmare to live with, since if I am talking and then am distracted, my train of thought will be lost and I will have forgotten what I was saying. I therefore butt in, to add my thoughts and the rest of the family have to wait because their memories can wait, whilst mine cannot; consequently we all talk at the same time. The one who talks the loudest obviously has the best point and is the winner!

My children used to tell me off when driving, as I would stop in mid sentence to concentrate on the driving, but a minute later would have forgotten what I was saying and then a few minutes later it would come back and I would be able to continue, even though by that time we would be onto another topic. I would go to a lecture or a church service and on the way home, my wife and I would be analysing what we had heard. My wife would often comment on what I said I had heard, "but he did not say that, that is not the same message that I heard".

As I could not accurately remember, I would have put my own spin on the information given. It had triggered off my thoughts, which had gone wild and I made sense of it in my own way, but it probably was not literally what had actually been said. Did it really matter? Most of the time no, but sometimes it did and could be very embarrassing. I hear many instructors say, "I told them very clearly, but they took no notice". Did they really 'hear' what was being said, or did they put their own spin on it?

We now live at the bottom of a hill, so like most communities today, we drive our cars and hardly ever walk up the hill or meet our neighbours. To make sure we keep together as a friendly entity, each year we have a neighbourhood get-together when we have a 'progressive meal,' during which we go round each other's houses for one course of a meal and then move on to another, and then another and finally end up all together for coffee and drinks. Some people know everyone's names, but I would like them to display a badge showing their name, the names of their children, their house number and the make of their car. When the jig saw has come together, I then know them and feel less embarrassed, but I still make mistakes. It is a struggle for me and, like some people, I could make an excuse not to take part, but that would defeat the object of having a meeting for everyone, so I try my best to cope at being sociable.

Now it could be thought that my terror at the thought of dancing was as a result of my repressed puritanical upbringing where dancing was regarded by some as 'a sin', or then again it could be put down to my natural lack of rhythm and inability to remember sequential moves, but I think it was a mixture of all these factors and that if I had had a good dancing teacher, who had understood my psychological reticence and physical problems, then I could have overcome the history, enjoyed the activity and then succeeded. I believe the same holds true when learning to drive. What has formed our responses in the past can be overcome with analysis, understanding and appropriate teaching, but if that is not done, then the learner's attempts just end in failure, because the issues have been compounded, rather than solved.

I hope this gives some understanding of why I have empathy for students who tell me "I don't work to systems," or "I don't do judgment," or "I can't follow instructions," or "I can't remember." It does not mean they cannot succeed. It just means that another way must be found around their problems. If one does not have a right leg, then they may learn to use their left leg to accelerate, but more importantly, it is obvious to others, so they can show understanding; but if there are perceptual or memory problems, it is not obvious and one has to learn to use other strategies which can then often be misunderstood. That is why, when driving, it is so essential that if they cannot judge, that they learn to use their mirrors and if they cannot remember the system, then the system is simplified, with them being helped to learn to perform the process instinctively.

People termed as 'lazy,' are probably making a great deal more effort than those who do not have any problems. This is because they have to devise their own ways to learn, whilst the 'hard workers' can just absorb the information which is presented. It has caused particular problems to those who are struggling to pass the recently imposed more difficult Theory Test. They feel they are constantly being tricked by inappropriate questions, phraseology and words they do not understand, which have no relevance to road safety.

It is not a small problem, but it is a hidden one and the driving schemes and driving tests should recognise and make allowances for these people with these specific problems. There are probably many more people with perceptual or academic problems who need to drive, than those with physical problems. It is hidden, because of the embarrassment of the individual and the lack of motivation by the Driving Standards Agency to recognize the depth of Disability Discrimination within the system. This needs to be tackled immediately. There is more to disability than physical disablement.

****

I hope these personal revelations of a few of my own 'brain malfunctions,' will give others the encouragement to admit; 'that is just like me', or 'I always thought I was stupid and the only one who had that problem.' There will be others, who will not have any personal understanding of what I have written, but this section may have focused their minds to recognise other problems they might have.

Have these problems affected my driving ability? No, I have just had to find another way to succeed. What I am highlighting is that everyone is different and teachers and driving instructors must get into the mind of the learner and not presume the person is either lazy or stupid, just because they do not think in the same way or have a problem recalling what they have been 'told.' If someone fails to learn, it is usually the teacher who lacks understanding of the problem.

Section 2 Driver Education

i) Learning Model.

ii) Learning Styles.

iii) My Way.

iv) Ownership to Competence.

v) Developmental Driving.

i)   LEARNING MODEL

I don't want this to become too technical, so it may help understanding if I explain it in sequential form. In the usual model of learning to drive, the Driving Standards Agency has the primary influence. It governs the System, the Approved Driving Instructors, the Learners and the Tests and then goes on to control Pass Plus. The client comes last in the hierarchy and if the DSA has got it wrong for that particular client, then it leads to failure at one stage or another. It is a cycle beginning with the DSA and ending with the DSA, which of course the client and the instructor are paying for. Client ownership is not a priority and the emphasis lies on whether a pre determined box is ticked at a designated time.

****

The **DSA model** is a full cycle of the DSA in control.
DSA Training System →DSA- ADI →Client →DSA-Tests →DSA- Pass Plus →The drivers are now left alone to cope in the best way they can and try to learn to take ownership.

The DSA tells the ADIs what to do and they in turn tell the Learners what to think and what to do. The ADI is the Servant of the DSA and the wishes and learning styles of the Client are incidental, so the learner may struggle to do something which is foreign to their nature and experience.

****

In the **LEARNER model**, the client is in control from the beginning to the end of the cycle. They come with their life experiences and end up with those experiences being developed and enhanced. Right from the start, ownership is vital and they never lose control of their own learning. It works like this; a full cycle of the client in control.

Life Experience →ADI aiding the client's Personal Driving Development →DSA Tests adapted to the Clients requirements →Personally designed Pass Plus →Continuing Personal Development and Ownership.
The Driver is in charge of continually developing their own skills.
The ADI is the servant of the Learner and since the learner is paying, their wishes and their learning styles are of paramount importance and they learn well because they understand, are supported and so quickly succeed in developing a high level of proficiency.

****

Under the first model the instructor imparts the DSA systems. The ADI acquires prescribed knowledge and is regularly checked in that knowledge; they instruct in that knowledge and then supervise and fault-identify the same knowledge within their clients. As it is external to both the instructor and the client, when something goes wrong, as it invariably will, they may display a lack of flexibility of thought. As it is only an acquired tool, in a crisis, they can regress to their basic instincts of control and out of frustration resort to the shouting and the inappropriate methods which we hear about so often. Many clients fail to succeed when the DSA system is the primary force, under which the ADI is acting as a DSA robot and imparting instruction and supervision, because the Learner's needs are being ignored or shown to be of little importance.

****

In the second model, the ADI works in a client centred way, because they believe it to be the correct way. It is an internalised belief and because the ADI is developing the skills of the learner, there is no need to get angry or feel stressed when there is a problem. They just have to find a different way to help them discover an appropriate solution and then draw on their own expertise to communicate this to the Learner. Their job is to provide a personalised service and to be an information resource for all the client's questions of: Who? When? What? Where? Why? How? and to guide them along the correct pathway towards acceptance by the DSA. Of course it must always be recognised, that if they have severe problems, they may not be able to attain the academic level or safety standards set.

****

It is obvious that I lean towards the primary force being the Learner, with the ADI guiding the learner and last of all the limited influence of the DSA, only when the client is ready for test. It is often forgotten that the DSA works for the Learners and the ADIs and not the other way round. Like the client, instructors also pay the DSA for its services. It is our Service Provider and not our Employer. Again I must keep emphasising the point that neither way is wrong, it just may be that one way is unsuitable for a particular client and the individual learner should have the choice as to how they are taught. Together with the instructor, the learner needs to decide what is best for them and as it is a client based partnership, they need to decide what balance they should work towards, since a total emphasis on either side is likely to be inappropriate.

The first model concerns me because the DSA has to be self financing and so we have to be wary as to the level it sets the fail rate. If these were GCSE or A level results, then the standards would have been continually rising, but it does not matter how hard the instructors work or what standards the learners reach, they will always succeed around the 42% variance rate, because the DSA is in control of the pass rate. The goal posts are constantly changing to make the tests more difficult and of course there is always the emotive excuse of Road Safety which the Government can fall back onto in order to defend their actions.

****

One might ask why, when high academic standards are flaunted by the Government, the DSA standards are allowed to remain so low. The answer is of course, that it would not matter how good the ADI's were, it is the examiners who pass or fail the clients under the DSA control. I think we might not be too far off the mark if we link pass rates with the Government's hidden anti car policy, but it is still up to the instructors to make sure they continue to raise the standards and help learners view the present system with open eyes, rather than be held down to a statistically regulated level.

ii) LEARNING STYLES

I taught a very bright vivacious girl who was a natural driver, so it surprised me that she was having extra tuition for her A-level maths and enquired why this was necessary. Her answer would not have surprised me if it had come from an average student, but from someone of her calibre, who ended up getting five 'A' grades at A-level, it did surprise me. "I cannot learn from one of my math's teachers". I pressed for further enlightenment. "She goes round the class, asking questions and I don't like talking in class, or learn like that. It embarrasses me. If I am going to get the "A" I need, I will have to go to another teacher who teaches me how I like to be taught."

Here was a highly intelligent student being failed by the system, because she did not learn in the way the teacher taught. I thought back to my many attempts to learn a foreign language at various stages in my life. I always gave up, because I could not answer out aloud. That was not my purpose for being there, or how I learnt. It may have been the teacher's brief to teach conversational German, but I just wanted to listen and pick up what I could for the purpose I needed. I can, even today, remember some of my embarrassments and the reasons for my decision to give up learning. How sad. I am sure my teachers had no idea why I actually left their groups. The motivation was there, the ability was there, but the teaching was inappropriate for me, so I never learnt.

The inappropriateness of questioning some clients was reinforced when a Supervising Examiner was making one of his periodic examinations of my 'teaching skills,' in what is known as a Check Test. I was marked down for not persisting in questioning one of my elderly ladies when she was obviously getting embarrassed. I had been aware of her increasing discomfort at the required questioning, which was only being used for the purpose of the test and not for her benefit; so when I responded in the interests of safety, by supplying the answer and moving on, I was penalised. The DSA expects ADIs to rigidly use Question and Answer Techniques, which may sometimes be relevant, but often are not, so I had only introduced the questioning to the lesson to enable the examiner to tick that particular box. It had no relevance to the situation, nor would I in my professional judgement have used it, but as there is no box to tick for professional judgement, I had to use it in order to try to get my grade. The examiner was compelled to fill his box, so both the sensitivity of the client and my professionalism was sacrificed for the sake of a tick in the examiner's box.

The lower grade I was given for this 'error,' had implications for the next 4 years of my disability instruction and assessment work, which is another indication as to why Check Tests are outdated and irrelevant for experienced instructors. If he had been able to ask me the background as to why I had made my particular decisions, especially as the time before I had received maximum grading for demonstrating my proficiency in this skill, then we could have had a professional discussion, of value to all concerned. I do wonder what understanding and teaching experience the Civil Servants who created these boxes have actually had and what depth of training the Examiners have had in Learning and Teaching Styles.

The driving behaviour of learners is primarily determined by three factors;
i) Biological; the presence of physical handicaps and minimal brain damage, which determine whether a person will be capable of driving normally, or if with certain modifications, they could become able to drive safely.

ii) Environmental; which encompasses both the social environment and the physical circumstances of location, finances and motivation.

iii) Psychological; which involves the learners' attitudes, self belief, experiences and expectations.

An understanding of the psychological influences is paramount to effective teaching, but it is an area usually ignored and is the one which ADIs, unsuspectingly, have to confront every day of their working lives. It is not the purpose of this section to consider any psychological studies, but just to convey that everyone learns in a different way and everyone teaches to their own strengths. An understanding of the reality of this and also the ability to adapt is essential to good teaching. David Kolb in his Learning Style Inventory based on his observation of people's behaviour, listed these as being; The Diverger, The Assimilator, The Converger and The Accommodator and categorised the Patterns of Learning into Concrete Experience, Active Experimentation, Abstract Conceptualisation and Reflective Observation.

****

As a Concrete Experience man and therefore primarily a Diverger, this is mostly beyond my thinking and putting people into boxes and categories has no place in my attitude to life. I just know that we are all different, we all learn differently and I try to act on that fact when I am teaching.

iii) MY WAY

If I asked a group of people how they learnt to do something, we would get a total mixture of methods and sequences. Some would have taken the traditional sequential pathway, whilst others would have achieved success by a variety of individual methods, which may have seemed so odd as to leave the majority of us scratching our heads and wondering how they achieved such success from the direction from which they came. My order of mobility was crawl, walk, three wheel bike, two wheel bike, car, van, bus, motorbike. For me, probably because of parental fears, the motorbike came last. I jumped from road sense on a pedal bike, to learning road sense in a car and then, when I had obtained considerable driving experience, I took up motorcycling.

On the other hand my wife was terrified of riding a bike, because of a transferred fear instilled by her parents, so she never successfully rode a bike. As part of her teacher's training course, she had to research how she acquired a new skill and chose to analyse how she would learn to ride a pedal bike. It was not wholly successful owing to her learnt fear, but she did appreciate the problems associated with mastering a new skill. Her sequence was crawl, walk, cycle and car. It did not actually matter that she was not a proficient cyclist, because she was able to miss out a stage and move on to learn how to drive a car? It is often mistakenly assumed that if a person has not attained proficiency in one skill, then they will not be capable of moving on to the next stage in the imposed sequence.

One woman explained to me how she had spent ten lessons learning cockpit drill and moving off and a further twenty lessons moving out of junctions. Her instructor would not let her progress onto the next stage, until she had perfected the set stage on his sheet. Needless to say, it slowly dawned that this was not the way to teach and she felt very negative towards instructors, quite angry, believing she had learnt very little and yet had spent a lot of money, time and effort.

I can remember watching my son learn to walk. At around nine months, having not crawled, he stood up by a chair, steadied himself and walked. It was just as simple as that. I can remember watching my daughter learn to walk. She shuffled, she crawled and then at sixteen months stood up, took a few steps, fell down and tried again and again. Over a period of months, she learnt to be a competent walker.

I watched my son learn to ride a bike. It was his fourth birthday and we bought him a two wheeled bike with stabilisers. He looked at it for a day and then demanded the stabilisers were removed. He wheeled it a few yards and kept looking at it. The next day he still looked at it, but to my disappointment, however much I encouraged him, he made no attempt to ride it. On the third day he came down and pronounced, "I am going to ride my bike today." He got on it, rode off down the street and never looked back from that day to this. He learnt by watching, getting his head round the issue and doing it. It was essentially a cerebral process. My daughter on the other hand used the stabilisers, had us holding on to steady her, fell off, a few tears and bloody knees and gradually in time she became confident. My daughter is now hardly ever off her bike, but she learnt in a completely different way to my son, who now rides motorbikes. She learnt by practical experimentation and responding to and learning from the knocks she received; the mind hardly came into it.

It was not for me to dictate, nor to even advise how they each achieved their goal; because my way would have been wrong for them; just as their mother's way with her learnt inhibitions, would have also been wrong. Any help given by me to my son, such as when I fitted the stabilisers, was regarded as inhibiting and therefore became downright dangerous. My role was to be there to suggest and protect from a safety aspect, but not to influence his developmental learning. On the other hand my daughter welcomed and needed the direct help, advice and support. Neither was right nor wrong. They just needed a different way of assisting their learning. My job as a parent was to be there to find the correct balance.

When we come to professional instruction, we often turn our backs on our instincts and do it as we have been trained; how the DSA wants, or the Education Department, or the Medical Board and of course we often get it wrong, because the individual does not easily fit in to the 'one size for all' system.

A large number of children and adults cannot read, because they did not learn by the system or method expected of them. It was not that they could not learn to read and probably would have learnt by using a different method which was more appropriate to them and which allowed their natural skills to develop under adult specific guidance.

In the same way, there are numerous people who cannot drive because of the way they have been taught, but are perfectly capable of becoming good drivers given a different way of learning and a different instructor. The problem mostly stems from inappropriate training by the ADI trainers and the wrong assessment values of the DSA. Once the ADI has been trained and a very difficult and expensive training it is, then they understandably think that is the only way and they become protective of their expertise and talk in jargon. There is no need for it to be so expensive or complicated, but it just propagates the myth of the mystery of learning to drive.

We now rely on experts in most walks of life, but instead of making life easier for us all, they both deliberately and unwittingly turn even the simplest learning into a complicated problem. The learner is overwhelmed, probably cannot understand and so does not enjoy and consequently does not learn. Subconsciously, these experts now feel they have to demonstrate their expertise and show how good they are, when what the learner really needs, is for them to keep it simple.

It happens in all walks of life and when I was recently in hospital I observed the same phenomenon within a different discipline. The patients were spoken to from a medical perspective and when they did not understand the jargon, the nurses, with the best of intentions, just repeated the same, but a little louder. It was not deliberate, nor unkind, but the professionals were coming at the problem from a professional standpoint, to which the patient could not relate. If the nurses had started to address the concerns from the patient's point of view, the patients would then have been in a position to 'hear' the professional reasoning, which they were being 'told'. As it was, the staff got more and more frustrated at the patient's inability to understand what they were trying to explain, so they raised their voices, because they were so keen to impart their message, but the more they spoke, the more their attempts at communication failed. I observed that the most successful at achieving this communication, was often the trainee, who was still in the midst of their own process of learning.

What staff needed to do, was to approach the problem from the perspective of the lay patient and then the message would be understood. Quite often the 'school failure,' is the one who finds a niche in caring for young children, because they actually understand what is required in being a good teacher. They have empathy, which all the highly trained and academically successful professionals cannot relate to.

Maybe they have just forgotten how to relate, or their natural communication skills have been trained out of them. Unfortunately the natural skill of the PDI (Potential Driving Instructor) is not always recognised, because the system wants those trainees to think in the same way, to enable them to be controlled more easily. What we urgently require as instructors are the 'driving failures,' who have found it difficult to learn to drive, because these are the ones closest to understanding the problems of the learners. Academic or skill qualifications may just get in the way and have little actual value, especially if they lead to being 'experts'

Experts sometimes try to make everything complicated, partly because it emphasises their own self worth and also as a need to defend their expertise. In fact most things are simple to understand if put into simple language and it is the art of the teacher to stimulate interest and provide the skills to access a complicated subject and to make it seem easy.

I am always keen to learn from anyone who can teach me, but having attempted most mechanical or constructional tasks at an amateur practical level, it can be quite amusing when I get the 'tut-tut' and the raising of the eyebrows, because the expert thinks his knowledge is too superior to be able to impart to someone as lowly as myself. I can hear the thinking, "Tut-tut, it's very complicated, you would not understand." The only reason I would not understand is because they deliberately make it too complicated, or are too poor as teachers to simplify the process to help me understand.

Once they have made it complicated, the more they believe they can then defend their expertise by making it even more complicated; but, the more expert they become, the less communication skills they usually have. What they need, is to become experts in how people learn about their subject, rather than knowledge of their subject.

****

A similar situation is developing in driver training and whilst most other experts can then of course charge more for their expertise, the overwhelmed ADI system means completely the opposite as very few instructors can now even make a reasonable living and the really experienced practitioners are being forced to leave what they regard to be their chosen profession. Driving Instruction must be one of the few professions where trainees do not have to reveal to their clients that they are just beginners and even when they are only partially qualified they can actually charge the same as highly experienced instructors. Trainee Medics are introduced as students and the permission of the patient is required.

iv) OWNERSHIP to COMPETENCE

In preparation for becoming an ADI, I taught my son and daughter to drive. She expressed concern about her friend's driving ability and asked me to advise her because, although she had passed her test, she was still terrified to drive. Fortunately my daughter had not experienced any such problems and as soon as she passed her car test, she asked to be taught how to drive our camper van and then how to tow the caravan. She followed this by taking her friends away in the caravan towed by the camper van and enjoyed the first of many wonderfully liberating holidays. It became such a feature of her girl friends' teenage experiences that, when one was having her hen-party, she asked to use our camper van in order for the 'posse of girls to relive their youth'. I am sure the stories that van could tell over its twenty two years would have to be censored!

When my daughter took her Gap year in the States she was put in charge of a fleet of vehicles, because she was so competent and could 'drive with a stick.' I began to wonder why she did not have any fear and could drive anything in any situation, when apparently many of her friends who had been to professional instructors, were terrified of actually driving even their tiny little cars when they were on their own.

As I became more involved with driving instruction, it became clear that some instructors only taught their clients to pass the test, as required by the DSA and therefore spent most of the lessons driving around near the test centre. This meant that if the learner could follow the set driving format for 40 minutes and nothing went wrong, they would then be issued with their full licence. They were then entitled to drive quite large vehicles in a variety of hazardous situations, when many of them really had no competence in driving. They had only been taught how to fit into the required DSA boxes, which then gave them a licence to learn by experimentation and they were subsequently abandoned to teach themselves their own survival techniques, which they gained through their own experience. They had only learnt what they were instructed to learn, rather than encouraged to take ownership of the skills they were performing. Their instructors may have implied that they taught 'driving for life,' but some had never even been taught to drive at 70mph, or to negotiate bends or overtake safely on country lanes, or drive at night and yet they had still got their licences. Of course they knew **how** to turn the car round in the middle of the road, but had not been taught **when** this was applicable.

I was in a traffic jam the other day, when a young woman proudly displaying her P plates, demonstrated her skills at the Turn in the Road. She competently performed all 19 stages of the procedure whilst everyone patiently waited and I wondered why she had not been taught to use her common sense and go round the block instead. It would have been quite likely that her friend, to whom she was demonstrating her superior skills, may have failed her test for touching the kerb, even though she may have been a far superior driver. Which was the safest or most valuable skill to have learnt; the turn in the road, or the ability to choose the appropriate way to turn the car round?

This 'learn after test' procedure seemed to me to be an extremely dangerous way of teaching someone to become a proficient driver, yet except for the few who take part in Pass Plus, which is also a strictly controlled programme, it is actually how many people learn, - after they have got their licences. The immediate reasons for this can often be laid at the parents' doors as they will only pay for their children to get their licences, rather than learn to drive beyond the basics. It is no wonder there are so many accidents and so many lives are lost amongst our young drivers and those without the wider experiences of driving. There are no compulsory progressive stages of experience to be encouraged to reach, or organised educational or information programmes to access.

I have long advocated a graduated system of licensing, whereby the Examiner assesses the candidate and gives them a grade, rather than a pass or fail. Obviously if they drive dangerously then they will fail, since we cannot have danger on our roads, but the present system encourages "danger by inexperience". Students are used to Graduating in their school subjects and unless they are particularly bad, they do not pass or fail, they Graduate and the grade then controls what stages they are able to move on to. Maybe they would choose to re-sit at a higher level, which would be encouraged, but it would not preclude them from driving at a lower level, or after much hard work and expense stigmatise them with a 'fail' as happens with the present system.

There is too much carnage on our roads caused by young, inexperienced, fully licensed drivers and we need to deliberate to proportion the blame. It should not all lie on the shoulders of the young driver. I am not referring to the hoodlums who are anti-social and need dealing with in a different way, but the youngsters whose lives are devastated by the destruction they have inadvertently wrought through lack of knowledge and experience.

Who is to blame? Can we always blame the driver who maybe is languishing in prison because he was not trained adequately? He was then given a licence by an examiner, who was working to the DSA standards, but was not allowed to use his common sense and issue a relevant grade for the experience demonstrated, nor follow this up by advice as to how to develop those skills ready for success at the next grade. Can we blame the Instructor who is working to DSA standards and quality control methods? Like many of my suggestions this may be controversial, but I also hope it is common sense, as I do not think the test should only be black and white, a pass or a fail, but also contain an assessment and a grading.

I would keep the stick for the real miscreants, but offer a carrot, maybe of a larger car or an extra 10% on speed limits, to those who wish to attain a higher grade by undertaking extra training courses. This would be both a deterrent and a perk, since the Grade would be incorporated in a chip on their licence which would activate the Engine Control Unit and a small LED light system would warn other drivers and the emergency services of the driver's ability, to enable them to take appropriate care and also indicate to cameras the relevant restrictions. Any serious contravention of traffic laws would lead to demotion to a lower grade. The 'boy racers' would be so precious of their grading that they would actively strive to improve and retain their grade and be mortified if they were demoted. This would be much more of a deterrent than a fine or points which no one ever sees.

The timid driver would be able to obtain a licence, so that their chances of earning their livelihood or providing for their families would not be destroyed. As drivers aged or became infirmed, they could choose to do nothing and revert to the basic restrictions or opt for a higher grading, by proving their capabilities by means of an assessment. This would mean they would not have a test forced upon them and they could still remain independently mobile and so enable the necessities of life to be undertaken.

At present we have a formal instruction system of exactly how one is expected to learn, but unfortunately many people do not learn like that. These are the controls. That is the road. Here is the system. This is where you do your test and you do it like this otherwise you will fail. However good you are as a driver, or however experienced you are, you will fail unless you fit this narrow box. Once you have passed, you are classed as just as good as any other experienced driver in control of a lethal machine.

Every day, examiners say to candidates "That was a very good drive, but you have failed because you bumped the kerb and that is an error which might in another circumstance have caused a problem." or "You did not turn your head when you made your safety check." But the point is it didn't have any safety consequences, because the candidate used their all round awareness and perception, instead of just performing the specific nods required. I once accompanied and observed an excellent test, but the young father was failed for omitting the compulsory right shoulder observation when performing the parallel park. The highly respected examiner said, "You know there was nothing there, John knows there was nothing there, I know there was nothing there, but there might have been!"

The corollary is "You have passed, but you still have many areas of weakness, although you did not make the errors which are described as serious mistakes on the prescribed sheet." It is not the examiners being difficult, since they are required to fit the client into the corresponding boxes, rather than make a relevant box for the client. They are not encouraged to use their common sense, although in fact some examiners are wise enough and experienced enough to be flexible in their decision making, but not all. I am sure all instructors have taken the almost perfect driver for test, who has then failed on some inconsequential judgement that we could all make every day we are driving, whilst another, who cannot think for themselves and can barely control the car has passed, because they have been too cautious to make errors.

Here is your licence, get out on your own and learn by making your own mistakes. No more guidance, no more help, no one to turn to. It is up to you. It's your time to sink or swim. Some wise learners opt to take the Pass Plus course, but that is also a highly regulated tick box DSA scheme where flexibility is discouraged and after one session on the motorway, or one session driving at night, the new driver will be told they have either 'Attained' or 'Exceeded' the standards required. Then we get the few, who choose to take further study and join various driving associations, such as the Institute of Advanced Motorists or Diamond Drivers, or ROSPA, but the numbers who join are very few and the courses do not always have the street credibility or incentives that the schemes deserve, so the majority of new drivers ignore the opportunity and hope for the best. They have their pink licence so the system believes they must now be competent until they reach seventy years of age.

One of the first things new drivers comment about when they are on the road, is that very few experienced drivers follow the indication rules, especially when negotiating roundabouts and so they are constantly confused and terrified. There is little understanding of the procedure amongst drivers and no enforcement. I wonder what has happened to the Road Safety Information campaigns we used to have. These newly licenced drivers then try to become part of the mass of moderate, bewildered and inexperienced drivers and within a few weeks, in the sink or swim atmosphere on our roads, they have also stopped doing most of what they have been instructed to do.

For the rest of their driving lives, no one checks them, or advises them, or offers development of their skills; unless of course they drive at a few miles over 30 mph; probably because they are concentrating on the numerous problems with which they are trying to cope. Under the New Driver Act, they then have to start all over again with new licences, new tests and probably more basic lessons. No incentive, no development, just punishment. I am not against appropriate punishment, but we all hear of the ridiculously low sentences for death and excessive speed; yet drive at a little over 30 and the punishment for the new driver is enormous and way beyond the bounds of reason when taken into context with the rest of the lax and reckless driving encountered, because standards are not being enforced. Of course, anyone driving without licence or insurance or recklessly, needs severe sentencing; but a loss of attention caused by inexperience, should in my book be treated by the opportunity of further training in ownership and not by the punishment of being regressively forced back to elementary driving.

****

As my theories have developed, I have realised that the Ownership should come right at the beginning of the learning process and that Competence comes towards the end of the process. Ownership comes from the brain and competence comes from the learnt skill. If it is taught the wrong way round; as we are encouraged to do at present; then many people get their pink with no ownership ability at all, so when the instructor has left the scene, the new driver is left floundering and often sinks emotionally or even worse has the serious accidents we hear about in our daily news bulletins. The easier to drive our cars become, the more important it is to focus on ownership rather than skills. Ownership is the ability to act appropriately on ones own, in a crisis, without stress, and without feeling the need for support. The present test does not adequately assess this area of competence.

v) <u>DEVELOPMENTAL DRIVING</u>

I have already discussed my view that we should be concentrating more on Developmental Driving than on Driving Instruction, but I need to explain how I implement this in my day to day work. I believe driving skills start to develop from a very young age with the developing attitudes and abilities of the child. These are further influenced by the personal experiences and environment of the individual. During the initial lesson it is necessary for me to assess these factors and discuss them with individual clients.

At first, I am not going to teach them anything in a formal way, nor do I enter the lesson with any pre conceived ideas of how the lesson will develop. My primary aim is to relax them; see if we can get on together; see if they need me and if I want to teach them and to assess what they already know and to recognise the skills they have already established which we can use to transfer to their driving.

Many of the factors involved in driving do not need to be taught, because as the learners have already had at least sixteen years of experiences, (some disabled may be licensed at 16) they have already developed their own strengths which have become a natural instinct to them. I took a girl with disabilities out for her first lesson and commended her for her very definite look over her left shoulder when she signalled left, as she was about to change lanes to exit a roundabout. She expressed surprise at my comments, since to her it was common sense and then she went on to explain that as she normally sat in the passenger seat, it was self-preservation to check if anything was about to hit her on the left.

The same happens when moving away; they usually look over their shoulder and do not have to be told to make sure the road is clear. Some may only use the mirror, but as long as it is safe observation, the issues of hidden views can be taught in later lessons as a matter of educational discussion. For some new drivers, the physical difficulty of twisting right, in order to make a shoulder check before driving off, is at this stage counter productive. It can result in the engine stalling as the left foot automatically lifts off the clutch and can end in consequent panic and the subsequent feeling of failure, when the action was actually unnecessary in the first place.

On first meeting my client, it is important to prioritise what is necessary and at this stage gears and clutch are not required, but it is vital to understand steering, road systems and the actions of other road users and to enable me to assess their ability to cope with speed, positioning and spatial awareness. For this reason everyone starts on the automatic car and because of the semi rural location where I live, the first drive is of around thirty miles of very varied driving.

This drive is largely free from stress since I have the dual control brake and I am in control of the car. I know that no one is going to do anything dangerous and we can begin at the beginning and add or develop their personal skills as they become able to accept ownership. I do not tell them what they should be doing, or give them any rules or regulations for them to try to remember, or overwhelm them by telling them what is obvious to them. Together we are going out for a drive and although I am always in control, they can take over whatever they feel they are capable of doing. If they miss an observation, I will make it for them, if they over steer, then I may give a slight correction towards the correct line.

Right away they drive off from where I pick them up and they are particularly excited if this is straight from home, because they have usually discussed what their friends did on their first lesson who were being 'instructed' and have some idea of the boredom that quite a few have encountered during their early lessons. I often get sad stories of instructors who have kept their new and enthusiastic drivers sitting by the side of the road, whilst they receive a long lecture on cockpit drill, until boredom has set in and I often pass learners sitting at the side of the road at the beginning of a lesson and find them still sitting there, saving petrol, when I return at the end of the lesson.

Amazingly, it is not only the learners who complain. I was recently surprised to hear one instructor bemoaning the fact that a lady had cancelled her booked lessons after complaining that she had been sitting at the side of the road for a two hour lesson, whilst he went over the cockpit drill and controls. As he explained, she had not appreciated that the car was his living and for the safety of others, he was not prepared to let her loose on his car before she understood all the safety procedures she needed to know.

I explain to my novice that my job is to develop the skills they already have and I know they have many of these skills in place through playing sport, riding a bike, skate boarding or pushing a trolley etc.

As it is their development we discuss, rather than it being my imposition of a system, they do not feel patronised in any way. Under my guidance, we drive through the town and out onto a fast country road presenting them with many bends, to enable me to assess their control and speed planning; we turn into a country lane with passing places where I am able to assess their spatial awareness and planning; then into a small town with a number of roundabouts where I am able to assess their steering and their understanding of negotiating roundabouts. I am not interested how or where they put their hands, just that they negotiate the roundabouts safely. If, like my girl with the disabilities, they can put in the appropriate indications as well as the over shoulder observations, then so much the better.

We progress to another town where there is a suitable housing estate for manoeuvres, which are executed under my guidance; the aim being to demystify the whole process. The first one we perform is the 'Turn in the Road', followed by the 'Reverse Round the Corner', the 'Emergency Stop' and finally the 'Parallel Park'. We return home, via the most complex six exit spiral roundabout in our area. They are exhilarated, overjoyed, raring to get going for the next lesson and I have a complete assessment of what I have to concentrate on developing and an understanding as to where they may have problems.

The second lesson is a development of the first, but introducing dual carriageways with seventy mile per hour speed limits and many fast roundabouts. At no time do I allow the learner to get stressed, or tired, nor to do anything they do not feel capable of doing. They know I am in control and they are developing their skills in a safe environment.

If they have not presented with any specific problems, then on the third lesson, I will introduce them to the manual with clutch and gears, but as they are now capable of driving in traffic and are not scared, they are ready and able to accept this introduction and can concentrate on the coordination demanded for gear changes whilst also paying attention to what is required on the road. Usually we will take the same circuit as the first lesson and as they are now conversant with the conditions, I just have to mention which gears to use and they change appropriately by themselves. By the end of the lesson, many are selecting their own gears as required, but as the lessons develop, I will reduce the prompts to see if they are thinking on their own.

I only try to intervene if they are doing something dangerous, but will not prompt, unless it is obvious they are not going to act on their own volition. For me to expect them to perform on their own, or think as quickly as I would do, is not required at this stage; the aim is that they actually do act on their own. For example, if they miss a mirror, it does not matter, because I have observed for them, or if their indication is not timed correctly, again it does not matter, because I have checked it does not have any implications to other road users. What I am looking for, is that they are thinking correctly by prioritising need and at this stage doing it skilfully does not really matter, since that is for a later stage of development.

If they do have specific problems, I may keep them on auto for much longer and some may choose to pass on auto and become proficient as drivers before tackling the gears. It is a decision we make together, taking into account all the issues which are relevant. No decision is imposed by me, although obviously I will advise if I feel strongly about which decision should be made. Once driving has been established and ownership accepted, I will provide them with as many different driving experiences as possible and lastly train for test and what the examiner will be expecting.

At first, this may seem a topsy-turvy way of doing it, but what I observe is that the candidate has already arrived at having the skills for themselves, because it has been their own personal development. If rules had been imposed or instructed, then the progress may have been very slow or even doubtful. But now the progress is established, the pernickety issues for test can be addressed and instead of them becoming a huge sequential mountain to climb and a mass of information to remember, the rules actually become absorbed as common sense.

We would not expect a student to take 'A' levels before their 'GCSE', and neither should we expect drivers to do the most difficult first. At a second glance it becomes obvious that the Driving Instruction System used at present is the topsy-turvy one and requires changing to make it more applicable to the needs of a modern clientele. My reasons for starting with an automatic car, have little to do with the coordination of gears and clutch, but with information processing and the prevention of overload. It is overload which causes stress, not gears or traffic. If, by first using an automatic we can reduce the brain processing required, then we will reduce the stress. If we reduce the stress, we will speed up the learning. It is so obviously a winning programme and over many years I have proved it to be a successful formula.

I taught one young woman who was very fearful of driving and knowing of the five failures her sister had experienced she requested to stay on the automatic. She was quickly successful and subsequently took only three lessons to transfer to the manual before she had also passed her geared test. Yes, she had taken two tests, but with very few lessons and no stress. Until I had appreciated the necessity for having an automatic car I used the same developmental principles on my manual car, but assisted, when appropriate, by using the dual clutch. There may have been an occasional smell of clutch burn, but it is a driving school car and the most important target in those early lessons is the fluency and safety of the drive rather than the precise control of the mechanics, or any emphasis on sequential processing. That will come easily, if the learner is relaxed.

I hope everyone passes first time, because this should mean they have money left to do The Pass Plus course and for me this further development after test is most important as they hone their skills whilst still under supervision and guidance. I am always disappointed if someone fails and their driving development is arrested, but so be it, and we then perfect what is required for the next test. I actually feel very disappointed if someone does not then take Pass Plus, because I think they really benefit from extending their experiences. With knowing the statistics of young deaths, I cannot understand why some parents, and even some instructors, do not see the need for this natural progression to Pass Plus.

I also always offer automatic experience for those who have come from other instructors for their Pass Plus course and who may have not previously driven auto. The understanding and safe use of, kick-down, gear selection, hill starts, overdrive, snow and sports modes and tip-tronic changes, are all invaluable for those who may have to hire in the States, or drive an automatic in this country. The night time session I offer is on pitch black unlit roads and if this means starting the lesson at half past ten at night because it is mid-summer, then that is what we will do. We negotiate severe hairpin bends on one of the windiest roads in Britain and usually encounter mist and weather changes at the highest town in the county.

Motorway driving is simple if it is straight driving and as that would be pointless I have devised a course, where the new driver experiences lane changes whilst surrounded by heavy lorries; the interchange of three motorways and also the entry and exit of various types of Service Station.

I believe the primary danger on motorways is the need to adapt to changing conditions, so we learn to exit from fast 70 mph roads onto narrow country lanes with passing places. If the client wishes to practise multi-storey car parking or brush up on some aspect they feel they are still having difficulty with, then that is also fine and I have even had those who have chosen to use hand controls as part of the Duke of Edinburgh Skills Course. I have never had anyone undervalue the experience they get and it is a further development of their driving skills and their Safe Driving for Life.

My aim is for us to begin at the beginning for that specific client and the lessons are then developed from where the individual has already reached and not from where I want them to begin, expect them to be, or where I want to take them. I had a very capable young woman who came to me after recommendation from her friends, because her confidence had been destroyed by the systematic methods which had been used to instruct her. It was totally against her personality, intelligence, experience and learning style, but she had received nine months of unnecessary instruction and cost, which had only restrained her natural development. Her instructor was excellent as an 'instructor', but that was not what she required. Once the reins had been relinquished, she blossomed and became the superb driver she should have been from the beginning. She did not need instruction, but just needed her innate skills developing.

****

I was talking to a German friend about the work I was doing and she said, "You are like a gardener." I actually thought this was the best description I have had of the work I do. I cultivate people's minds to enable them to develop their driving skills and hopefully prepare them to be able to cope with any situation which they may encounter when I am not sitting next to them. Every plant is different and requires different growing conditions; some are already seedlings when I get them and for those I must be careful not to kill the life that is already growing; some require special conditions to assist their development; some take a long time to germinate, whilst others grow rapidly. Some need to be hardened off before planting them out whilst others can be sown outside right away. As all the plants are different, if they are not handled correctly they will either die or develop inappropriately. The good gardener knows his plants and with careful nurturing will get the best out of them and by using different methods they will grow up to be sturdy and strong.

Section 3 Skills and Techniques

i)   Basic Skills.

ii) Skills Required.

iii) Developing Skills.

iv) Too Complicated.

v)   Teaching Dynamics.

i) **BASIC SKILLS**

I remember as a child being taken up Blackpool Tower and looking down from a great height at the trams, cars and people all going about their own individual businesses in perfect harmony. The trams were easy to understand, because they were guided by the rails and so followed a fixed pattern, but the people all seemed to be programmed to avoid each other and what was more amazing was that the lumps of metal many of them were sitting in were, irrespective of each other, all apparently under perfect control and safely wending their own particular routes. I wondered what unseen power was needed to make this happen and what would develop if they became unable to avoid each other?

Of course it is not quite as simple as that, since we are not dealing with a super power or an equality of experience and ability, but a mass of people who are all individuals, with their own strengths and weaknesses and whose driving becomes the great highlighter of need. A thespian I taught stated: "Learning to drive shines a spotlight on all your weaknesses." Whilst she could cope with the spotlight of the theatre and letting her interpretive personality shine through, it was a different experience when learning to drive within a system which controlled her. My job as her teacher was to develop her strengths and sublimate her weaknesses until they became in balance and subsequently merged in harmony with other road users. It is not easy.

On the positive side, learning to drive also reveals personal strengths and makes the individual understand that they do have those undiscovered strengths which had never before been recognised, since they had been just taken for granted. Unfortunately, one also has to face up to known weaknesses, but it does help to consciously acknowledge and list known strengths, so as to be able to counterbalance the previously hidden weaknesses which are now revealed and to recognise the new strengths which will be discovered. It is also a requirement of a driver to be able to relate to the possible strengths and weaknesses of other road users and realise they will be different to their own and so to drive defensively. The brilliant driver may drive as if everyone else is brilliant and on many occasions I have had to teach these 'clever' ones, to drive as if they are disabled, just to help them recognise the difficulties others may be facing, rather than getting irritated by their actions.

The instructor is not just there to point out the personal weaknesses and identify faults, since this can be destructive, but to help the learner discover and recognise these for themselves and decide how to find their own solutions. These are personal solutions and should not be the solutions imposed by the instructor, since the primary focus should be on developing the candidate's strengths, rather than imparting the ADI's driving strengths, which he is likely to believe are the ideal. The skill of the teacher comes in their ability to help alleviate these weaknesses without stress, but any repeated reference to failure, or repetitive analysis of faults will usually be counter productive. What is required is calm guidance along the paths of remediation, rather than confrontation with failure.

My childhood observations from Blackpool Tower still amaze me, especially now I understand how different people's minds are and how differently they function. Just how we avoid accidents is a mystery.

As the modern day traffic density has become so great, it is even more surprising that people can develop the skills to drive safely and pass their driving tests to become competent enough to drive with others. Knowledge of why people can drive and why some find it difficult, becomes only too obvious when the required skills are broken down and analysed and maybe this understanding would help some people to decide before hand whether they are going to have difficulties and what ways they could use to prevent those stresses leading to subsequent failure. By understanding the skills, it may help alleviate the effects if the actual problems become manifest, or why, if we disturb that equilibrium by illness, medication, or mental malfunction, we could experience chaos and disaster. If we looked more at how people function, rather than the system, then we would be on the right track to ameliorating some of these pressures.

****

Systems don't get depressed and act out of character, but people do and the overemphasis on understanding the system, rather than people, can be to the detriment of us all. The reason for failing or being a poor driver is not usually an inability to cope with the system, but because people are people and we need to understand how they will act and react. Driving is not a system, but an art and it depends on how one understands and relates to other drivers, which determines how good a driver one will become.

ii) SKILLS REQUIRED

In my next book, **DRIVING IS turning disability into ABILITY** I will consider the effects of disabilities in more detail, but list here a few of the factors affecting the acquisition of the basic skills. I emphasise that I do not have any professional medical knowledge, so anything I mention is through personal observation and may or may not have any validity. I am sure there is plenty of room for the individual reader to make their own amendments to this list. Anybody having one, or a mixture of these problems, does not necessarily mean there will be any consequences on their ability to learn to drive, but just that if there are problems, it may be necessary to look deeper. I have taught people with many obvious disabilities who have sailed through their driving and I have taught others, with what may have appeared to be only slight problems, but which have nevertheless had serious consequences on their driving. The main point is that as we are all different, we do not give up, but search to enable each of us to discover the specific ways which enable us to best achieve.

****

Co-ordination. Difficulty in this area can be a big problem, because of steering and the control of gears and clutch. It is often caused by an undiagnosed problem from childhood, when the nerve pathways have not been adequately developed. It is necessary to have the ability to combine all the factors involved in driving to provide a fluid, rather than a staccato response, but many may find this difficult, such as the Dyspraxic, who may have been a clumsy or messy eater, or an untidy writer, or who did not like sport.

Hand- eye co-ordination: Leg- eye co-ordination: Left and right balance:

Left and right differentiation Patterns and Angles: Visualisation of Geometrical Understanding Reversing

****

Awareness. Slowness in this area can be a major safety problem, especially when hindered by a timid personality, fear, medication, brain dysfunction, or background experiences.

Situation Awareness: Speed Awareness: Prediction: Observation:

****

Planning.   Lack of organisation, over planning, or panic because of poor planning.

Decision making: Speed of reaction: Smoothness of reaction:
Observation and seeing with meaning: Adaptability:
Flexibility and the ability to 'think on the run'
Reacting both quickly and appropriately: Problem Solving:
Sequential Planning:

****

Memory   Problems can be caused by forgetting or muddling instructors/examiner's instructions.
Auditory memory: Visual memory:
Sequential memory:

****

Concentration Disorders such as Attention Deficit Hyperactive Disorder (ADHD) or Obsessive Compulsive Disorder (OCD)
Switching   Prioritisation

****

Perception   What the driver understands may not be the normal reading of the situation

****

Relationship   Difficulty in relating to other road users. Autism, Anger, Road Rage. Too ordered, not liking plans to be frustrated.

****

Cognitive   Understanding Rules, Following Rules and Obeying them.

****

Reaction   Speed of thought, accurate interpretation and speed of implementing that thought in action.

****

FACTORS which can hinder a full ACQUISITION & MANAGEMENT of these SKILLS

Immaturity   Premature births or emotional immaturity.
****

Special Educational Needs   including Specific Educational Needs. e.g
Dyslexia, Aspergers.
****

Psychological Behaviour   I will just list a few issues.

Anger Management / Behavioural modification, Recognition and Control of Fear and the resulting Stress, Balancing the 'Fight or Flight' syndrome, Panic. Recognising and coping with hidden and conscious negative experiences; Flashbacks, Loss/Bereavement, Neurosis, History of failure, Depression, Emotional disability.
****

Psychiatric Behaviour   Often undiagnosed or unrecognised, but can have serious effects. Recognising and coping with the effects of;
Bipolar,   Psychosis,   Phobia,   Schizophrenia.
****

Medical   Medication or pain control which dull reactions.
Hormonal, which can affect reactions. Muscular weakness,
Pain, Diabetes, Epilepsy, PMT, Menopause
****

Impairment   Accident; Environmental; Infection; Genetics;
Birth Trauma; Congenital; Minimal Brain Damage;

Sensory impairment;   Hearing   Sight   Night Vision

Physical impairment;   Fine motor skills Gross motor skills

Mental impairment;   Brain damage
****

It is vitally important for learners and medics to know of instructors who are specialists in this area of work. Unfortunately a short course is not usually enough to gain the knowledge required, but many have come into instruction after years of previous professional experience. Please let me know of your interest.

iii) <u>DEVELOPING SKILLS</u>

The more I thought about how many skills were involved in learning to drive, the more the list developed and its length might by now have overwhelmed some readers, since they had never thought all those skills could be pertinent to learning to drive. It is also important for the instructor to have a knowledge base of these factors. Sometime we get learners who have all the relevant skills in place before reaching the driving age and most instructors will have taught those who have quite easily passed their test from scratch in ten lessons. We use the term 'born drivers,' but what we mean is, that over their seventeen years of life, they have developed the required skills and practised them, so when they come to drive, it is just one or two additional skills to be added to the many they already have perfected.

The suggestion of considering restricting licences until drivers have had a year's experience seems to be another bureaucratic lack of understanding of how people learn, since some have already had many years of experience, whilst others are just beginning to develop these skills from scratch. I taught one academically very slow young man to pass his test in seven lessons and when I expressed my surprise at his skill, he answered, "well I cut the lawn." Of course what he meant was he used a sit-on mower, so there was very little else to learn to add to his years of already developed experiences. His road skills were impeccable because he had observed what his parents did and he had learnt by observation to make his own correct decisions. I taught one young woman with severe ME who was physically very weak, but passed with ten lessons. When I complemented her on her ability she said "well I have driven a wheelchair for years". Both used transferable skills.

If one is lacking in one or more of the listed skills, it can make the difference between being quick to learn to drive or taking a considerable time, but all is not lost, since many of those skills can be strengthened away from the car. There may have been an arrested stage of development at childhood and therefore some of the child development games can still be used to stimulate the brain.

It often happens that because the child had difficulties with a particular activity, e.g. those children who had poor coordination with ball games, then they were sidelined or chosen last for the team, so as a defence, they chose to avoid those activities, which in fact were the ones they needed the most help with. Isn't it typical that the ones who need the help are usually ignored, whilst all the effort and opportunities are given to those who don't need it because they already have natural ability? Many of these strengths can be developed at home, so I mention just a few to help discussion.

****

Developmental games:

i)   'Simon Says:' is ideal for developing the ability to respond quickly to the instructions of the examiner to help to overcome the delay in processing the information. Some examiners give too little time for the learners to process the information, but most soon perceive the candidate's problems and adapt their timing of instructions.

ii)   'Snap:' can be used to quicken up responses and is particularly useful for those who may be too hesitant at making decisions.

iii)   'Pairs:' to help memory and to identify and understand shapes, position and form.

iv)   'Directions:' to help follow instructions and to develop sequential memory.

v)   'I spy:' to develop observational skills and the speed of response to what is happening around.

****

<u>Practical activities that can be used to develop skills;</u>

i)   - pushing a trolley around a supermarket in order to develop control and spatial-awareness.

ii)   - ball games- catching, throwing and kicking to develop eye-hand-foot coordination.

iii)   - turning a steering wheel, a plate, or even a round washing up bowl when using both hands.

iv)   - using a toy car or matchbox to practise parking between two mats. As a child I used to build garages out of dominos and try to park my car in them without knocking the wall down.

v)   - sitting on a stool and planning all the mirror and shoulder check sequences as if moving off or stopping.

vi)   - standing at a roundabout and contemplating what drivers should be doing, rather than what they are doing, can be extremely beneficial to develop an understanding of roundabouts, before having to face those complexities whilst also trying to control the car

vii)   - observing the position of the wheels of the cars on a roundabout to determine whether they are exiting and should be indicating, or whether they are continuing on around.

viii)   - sitting on the upstairs of a bus and mentally making the decisions which they think the driver should be making.

ix)   - sitting as a passenger and observing and commenting on what they would do and seeing if the driver makes the same decisions. This can of course be done in silence within the head, to prevent conflict between the observer and the driver!

x)   - one student explained how she trained herself not to lose focus when doing the Theory Test by switching the television on in order to distract herself when practising. She programmed herself to be able to function with a background distraction without losing concentration.

This is not a patronising list of activities, since it could save hundreds of pounds, as well as much despair. I feel so sad when I read on the net of learners who have taken their test ten or fifteen times or meet those who come to me after suffering in a similar way, when neither they, nor their instructor, has identified their problem, nor put an appropriate remedial programme in place to rectify the problem. Too often I hear; "he just shouted at me;" or "we just carried on doing the same thing every week;" or he said "Practice makes Perfect and you will get there in the end;" or "Positive Mental Attitude" (PMA). If all these lead to more failure, then surely it just compounds the feeling of failure.

My question is always, "What do they think you are paying them for?" Many of us do not learn by being told and it is not war time where needs determine there is a quick selection process and those who can, do and those who cannot, don't. I have taught young men and women who a few generations ago I would have put them in a Tiger Moth or a Spitfire after only a few lessons and sent them off on their own to defend our country, but there are many others who would never have got off the ground. Times have changed. The need for most people now is to be able to drive, irrespective of their natural ability and it is the job of the instructor to facilitate that need and make a licence a safe reality.

* * * * * * * * * * * * * * * * * * * *

Instead of all the negativity that is often given to people with problems, think of the problem as a practical opportunity and turn it into a positive by finding and developing a solution. The client should take control of their own learning, by first recognising if they have the skills in place to learn to drive quickly, or whether they need to develop those skills before coming for lessons. It should not be a one way responsibility totally in the hands of the instructor, but a joint development in the hands of the learner, but under the guidance of the teacher.

iv) **TOO COMPLICATED**

I believe the DSA teaching model starts from the wrong base. Instead of beginning at the beginning and developing natural understanding, it starts at the finished article and the learner is presented with the whole scenario to which they have to attain. Of course the student response is quite appropriately, "boring, boring" or they just switch off. At first they come to their lesson with incentive, but the method and the system presented to them stifles that enthusiasm and instead produces uncertainty, hesitancy and consequently danger. They are not allowed to develop at their own level, or use their own methods, but are moulded to use the DSA methods, or those of the instructor, which can be quite contrary to their personal good learning.

Instructors seem to be expected to present the new driver with a complexity of information, which at the time has no relevance to them until they themselves have also become experts and are then able to understand it. The mind becomes overloaded, then crashes and the enthusiasm can be lost in a flood of tears or disappointment. They have suddenly been presented with a huge problem which is largely unnecessary and of the instructor's making, rather than meeting the needs of the learner. One of the main reasons I am given for clients having moved from their previous instructor is that they were overwhelmed by the amount of information given, most of which was unnecessary and what often amounts to the instructor 'showing off' his knowledge without having any sensitivity as to what the learner required or could cope with. Quote from a young mum, "I wanted to scream and shout, 'I don't think like that, I don't know what you are talking about, just shut up and let me drive'."

Many instructors are frightened of using their own initiative, since they know they will be marked down by their Supervising Examiner and told they are no good if they use their own ideas, however successful those ideas may be. Just like my first headmaster, they dictate, 'This is the DSA system which you will follow'. Sometimes the unthinking Civil Servants may implement a comfortable system for them to control but, as they are not teachers, they do not even understand the problem they are pontificating about. Let's look at a few situations where, if the simple learning is tackled first, then the complex develops naturally with understanding.

The System expects the whole process to begin with the full advanced sequence in place. The theory is 'teach it all and the correct pattern will be instilled,' but that only can happen if the learner is not overwhelmed and has the kind of mind which works in that type of sequential manner.

****

Make it simple

Roundabouts present huge problems to new drivers, yet they are really quite simple. The reason for the problem is that they are taught back to front or from the top down, rather than from the bottom up. I have taken many terrified learners who have been overwhelmed by all they have been taught to sequence and have come to me absolutely petrified and unable to negotiate roundabouts, which has resulted in them either braking dangerously, or racing onto the roundabout because they have been unable to think and sequentially process the mass of information expected of them. What I do is to break the requirements down to the essentials, to enable them to concentrate on what is important for them as a learner and I pick up what they cannot cope with. The job of an ADI is to prioritise safety, whilst the priority for the learner should be to concentrate on their steering and the observation of where they are going, followed by their speed of entry and their decision to enter if it is safe to proceed. It felt really good when a seventeen year old with Specific Needs, on only her second lesson exclaimed, "I love roundabouts!" She had not been overwhelmed, so had not been stressed and realised that roundabouts are really quite simple.

I do not see much point in learning the rest of the sequence if they cannot negotiate the roundabout safely in the first place, so I have dual controls which I can use if the speed of entry or decision making is not correct. Then we put together observation, speed and position. Lastly, the icing on the cake for the driver approaching test is to ask, what is happening behind? This is a very advanced concept, since not only do they have to translate what is behind, from the reverse image viewed in their mirrors, but also learn to assess the speed, distance and positioning of following traffic. To many drivers, it is not even understood why so much emphasis is put on this sequence, since in an emergency stop we don't bother to look behind because we must prioritise the essentials, yet when teaching roundabouts, we are expected to present the whole perfect system as if we are teaching experts and it is not what is actually required.

One of the reasons it is so complicated is that it is as if one is rubbing one's tummy whilst patting one's head. The brain just does not do it effectively, so instead we have to break it down into two separate processes. To go ahead; look to the right then, turn the wheel to the left. As the learner gets more proficient, it is possible to almost synchronise the two together. Is it any wonder it seems so complicated and causes so much difficulty to our learners and wastes so much of their money when instructors, as part of imposing the set System, encourage the learner to feel overwhelmed and a failure? What the learner is trying to do is actually quite simple, if we did not complicate it too much.

I am not saying that the Mirror- Signal- Position-Speed- Look sequence is wrong, but that for some, it is taught in the wrong order. It should be Look-Speed-Position-Signal- and maybe Mirror and after achieving competence, they can then be presented with the finished article MSPSL. Would we teach a child taking its first steps to look behind when it is trying to step forward, yet this is what we expect from our learners and it leads to the failure, danger and terror of so many? The primary job of the professional ADI is to present these situations without fear and to keep the learner safe, by performing the required sequences for the learner, until they can use them for themselves and take control.

One of our childhood reprimands is, "look where you are going," rather than "look what is behind you". If one thinks of the complexities involved in looking in the mirror, it is obvious that many people just check their mirror as a movement of the head because it is required on test, but it actually means nothing to them because nothing registers. I was teaching mirror-use to one young woman and she explained that she thought it was pointless because she could only look at the back of the inside of the car and found it impossible to focus beyond and through the rear screen, because everything was muddled, reversed and confusing. Well obviously it is as it is all back to front. It is quite an advanced skill for some drivers to learn to transpose a mirror image, to actually understand what is happening behind the back of their car and by that time they have nearly crashed at the roundabout. Because it has been taught in the wrong order, many learners have learnt to just nod for the sake of the examiner, rather than it having any safety value. Like many aspects of the test, it becomes a pragmatic exercise, rather than one of safety ownership.

I have learnt by experience that when necessary, I should teach the entry to roundabouts in stages, but when I demonstrated this advanced technique on a Check Test, I was marked down a grade, because I was concerned with the brain function of my Cerebral Palsy driver and the examiner did not have a box to tick for understanding 'overload' or 'brain function' and so my teaching procedure did not fit the DSA system. The result of that 'error' and my consequently lower grade, could have seriously affected my work with my disabled clients because knowledge of my grade is always required by the Disability Agencies. The reason for my decision was not understood by the examiner, but there was no opportunity to discuss the reasons because my lower grade had already been allotted.

One Supervising Examiner advised me not to bring candidates with problems for Check Test, because they did not fit the criteria demanded. My response was that specialist examiners should be used who could fit the criteria demanded by these candidates, since they represented the type of work I undertook with those learners with Special Needs. I have asked for the formation of a team of Specialist Supervising Examiners who would be able to Check Test those who specialise in different areas of the work. The present Check Tests are a DSA control game, having little validity for experienced instructors and are actively detrimental to their clients, especially to those with any form of difficulties.

****

Positive Strokes

One of the DSA's priorities is 'fault analysis.' This again can be so destructive to the less confident learner who withers under the criticism and it can also produce an aggressive response from the more confident. "It was all negative. We don't need to be told our errors, we know them," is the comment I so often hear. Would we say to a child who has just fallen over whilst learning to walk; "you've done that wrong, you should be standing firmly on your left leg and then moving your right leg forward? "If you did it how I told you to do it, you would not have fallen over. Now do it again." Floods of tears would be the result and yet this is precisely what we are instructed to do. Rather than ignore the negative and instead give positive support, we are expected to fault analyse, so of course for many, we instigate the same result; floods of tears.

I believe some instructors teach a nineteen point sequence for the Turn in the Road. How anyone with sequential memory difficulties is expected to remember this is beyond me and of course it is totally unnecessary. It is actually a very simple common sense process if you just do one thing at a time and gradually merge the individual stages into a smooth sequence. Stop, Steer, Look and Move. Then multiply this three times. There will of course be those who then give a lecture on not using 'dry steering'. Why ever not if that is the way they learn! In time, they can develop into the experts we are. Then we get the thorny problem of mirror use. We are constantly drilling them into using their mirrors and then when it comes to reversing and they actually need to use their mirrors for positioning, some instructors say they cannot use them and must twist and stare through the rear window. Reversing is made so unnecessarily complicated and stressful. Obviously they require good-all-round-observation, but I sometimes wonder if it is a case of 'business is business'.

From a teaching point of view it is all topsy-turvy and from a learning point of view it certainly does not make sense. One does not start with the finished article and try to achieve perfection from the outset. One starts with the individual stages with which the learner feels comfortable, which in turn build to make a superior product. The system should start with the learning stage and not the expert stage. In one of my correspondences with the Chief Executive of the DSA regarding the difficulties that many less able students have with the complexities of the Theory Questions, I was informed that the DSA had 'consulted the experts,' in both the selection and language used. I realised that this was where it gets it so badly wrong since it consults 'experts,' instead of the people who are struggling.

****

What is being created by this rigid adherence to Systems is a driving force of unthinking robots, which then make mistakes because they are not driving for themselves but for a system, which they do not understand nor feel comfortable within. What is even worse, is that the emphasis on the negative, instead of on realistic but positive strokes, make many learners feel failures, hate their lessons and become too terrified to think for themselves. Most instructors are struggling to do their best for their trainees, but the experts have made it too complicated, instead of them really understanding how people think, act, react and learn. Let's just keep it simple. Let's find the way the individual learners learn best and teach them in the way which is the most appropriate for them.

TEACHING DYNAMICS

I am fortunate to be able to discuss most issues with my wife and we enjoy analysing many topics in depth. Why then did it all go wrong when my mother-in-law used to be present? We all seemed to have our own roles, agendas, histories and relationships which affected the interaction. When she had left us and we were alone again, then peace and harmony descended. It was quite real and afterwards we often used to question why we behaved in such an uncharacteristic manner, but in fact it was not only difficult to understand, but even more difficult to prevent. It was just something which happened and so to establish harmony we had to adapt our mode of behaviour and by trying to understand our different backgrounds and analysing why we responded as we did, we became able to moderate our behaviour.

I am sure you have all had teachers with whom you learnt very well and then the others when you felt you learnt nothing and hated the subject. There was nothing necessarily wrong with the teacher or the subject, just the interaction. I can remember one teacher who seemed to dislike me and so I led her a-merry-dance. I was regularly sent to the teacher next door for the strap, which was the instrument of punishment in my school, but the teacher chosen to impose the punishment could never understand why such a bright and diligent student for him, was so often having to be punished for her. I can also remember 'Miss Flaherty' who was beautiful and young, with an amazing soft Irish accent and as a young teenager I loved her. I wished the lessons would last for ever and so I used to seek more help than I needed because of the smell of her perfume and the look of her pure skin. She also imparted a love of Geography which has never left me!

There are many more factors involved than just driving a car and the relationship between the instructor and the learner is paramount. I am not saying there needs to be an attraction there, because even that could be a hindrance, but it is difficult to learn if there is something you do not like about the person and that may have nothing to do with the actual individual concerned, but may be governed by your own past experiences. It is then up to the instructor to recommend that the client seeks help from another instructor, or the learner parts company before the situation develops into animosity which would prevent effective learning.

Unfortunately as learners become scarce, there is the danger of 'client hugging,' where the instructor holds onto learners who they know they really should pass on. I have heard the term 'mortgage payers' used; these are the ones whom the instructor does not have the skills to teach, but for years still carries on giving them lessons. I really do appreciate the instructors who, when they recognise they are out of their depth, refer difficult clients for special help. This shows not only an understanding of the issues, but also a desire to do what is best for their clients and this is always really appreciated by the clients. I have never had a client complain about an instructor who has referred them, but I often do about those who have clung on and by so doing have contributed to the sense of failure.

Many years ago I was teaching my older sister and mother to drive. My sister was very much task orientated and just did what I told her, so she passed her test without any problems, but without much wider understanding or ownership. Some years later I can remember seeing her driving along near home and as I wanted her to give me a lift I waved frantically and almost jumped in front of the car in my effort to get her to stop. She still did not see me and drove past. When I confronted her with her lack of observation, she told me "I was not looking for you. I was concentrating on my driving." She demonstrated what I call 'mental tunnel vision'. She was totally focused on the task in hand and that is how she learnt. She learnt under her own terms and I just had to tell her what to do and she did it to the best of her ability and passed first time. At the time I had recently passed my PSV double-decker test, so I taught her to that standard and she just applied what I explained to her.

My mother on the other hand wanted to discuss, reason and argue all the aspects of every issue and as the mother/son relationship was making her learning to drive more difficult, she decided to go to an instructor. After a few lessons she confronted him with, "I am more frightened of you, than the driving." His response of, "that is how it should be," sealed his fate and the mother/son relationship seemed a better option than arguing with a stranger. She was personality orientated and could only learn if the relationship gelled. No way could she learn from someone she did not respect or was unable to have banter with. The task was just not worth it. Two members from the same family, but so different in their learning styles that they needed different approaches.

Sometimes family dynamics and driving just do not mix or maybe they can work with one member, but not necessarily another. I can remember one father saying to me "I thought she would be just like my sons to teach;" and I was amused to read a woman commenting on how driving changed her family dynamics. It went something like this;

"When I drive, my normally loving husband makes me feel incompetent and puts me so much on the defensive that I have to keep telling him how good I am. Can you tell me how long I get for murdering a partner?"

****

Everyone is an individual with different characteristics, fears, history, abilities and interactions. That is one of the main issues which influences how people learn to drive. We are human beings and not robots who can be taught in a set manner and it is up to both the ADI and the client to try to make that work. If it doesn't, then it will not be productive and the driving partnership must cease whether it be professional, family or friend and there should not be any animosity involved. There is no disgrace in changing instructor if you don't feel they are right for you. To continue will only make the problem considerably worse since it will make the driving seem stressful, when in fact it is the interpersonal relationship which is at fault and not the driving.

Section 4 Modes, Methods and Messages

i) Multi Sensory Approach

ii) Mode Switches.

iii) Erecting a Tent.

iv) Hidden Communication.

v) No Shouting.

i) MULTI SENSORY APPROACH

Some people struggle to learn the theory facts, or remember their sequential processing, so I will don my mortar board for this section. Let me give some basic pointers which may help learning for those with Specific Needs. We use our many brain receptors to learn and as these are situated in different parts of the brain, the most effective way of learning is to use as many of these receptors as possible. The stronger pathways will support the weaker ones and completely new pathways may be formed.

We use our senses to register this in our memory and the more senses we can use, the more we are likely to remember. Some people have **visual** strengths, others **auditory** strengths, whilst others prefer practical **action,** or even use their **tactile** memory to help them remember. It is always better if one can understand their own personal difficulties and then develop their own methods of remembering. If I give you my system, you will forget, because it does not belong to you and is not yours. I will just give some guide lines to develop. Most of us use a mixture of methods and connections which relate easily to us, whilst those imposed by others, or given by instruction, may be completely wrong for us.

I like to think there are six senses; hearing, sight, smell, touch, taste, and the most important one is common sense, which develops through experience. All the senses are being used together, so there is a constant cross over whilst they support each other and it is therefore necessary to look, read, say, listen, write and draw, to help establish a clear pattern through using as many of the senses as possible.

****

Strategies for Learning the Theory.

Seeing by using Eye function.

Look, repeat, register and remember. Use long, short and middle distance vision, scan or make the words or diagrams blurred in order to stimulate memory, as well as vision. Half close the eyes and only look through the eyelashes, or read through dark coloured glasses. Some dyslexics read much better by using coloured lenses or coloured transparencies, since the black print on white paper is less stark and therefore the letters appear less jumbled. Make progressive notes, or follow diagrams on worksheets. The message is reaching the brain through the eyes.

Listening by using Ear and Speech functions.

This can be done in various ways, such as reading aloud or recording onto a cassette recorder. Reading out aloud is quite different from silently reading within the head. Read and record onto a recorder and then listen to your own voice again and again and since different receptors are employed, it will register differently and more easily support the other processors. It is thought that listeners remember their own voice more easily than hearing the words of another. Personally I find it helps me to concentrate much better, because the message is reaching the brain through practical action. If I read in my head, then my mind wanders, but if I read out aloud, the physical action helps me to focus and concentrate on the words and their meaning.

Instead of just thinking the words through within the brain, or reading out aloud, cup the fingers around the ears and draw them downwards and with the palms around the chin divert the voice towards ears and chant the mantra. This works well, since your voice is also passing through the air, rather than just being conducted through the bone. Plastic aids are commercially produced to help this process. The message is reaching the memory externally through the air waves, internally through the brain and also conducted through the bone to the ears. Singing can be particularly helpful in stimulating the memory.

Touching by using Writing.

Write it down to use tactile reinforcement. Use different coloured pens or script and underline or highlight. Even different textures can help some, as children often learn by writing in the sand or in the air or on a carpet or sand paper. Practically doing things can also reinforce the patterns; especially chanting to rhythms and skipping, in order to practically reinforce the other senses. Don't just look at diagrams and plans, but draw round them to reinforce the memory patterns.

Tasting and Smelling.

Of course we could leave these out of this process, but should we, as it is not such a ridiculous suggestion? Some people do visualise sound as colour or patterns or numbers, so maybe taste and smell could also be triggered. The brain pathways cross over and our unique creativity is manifest because all our brains are different and they forge different links, which then make those people with the unusual differences stand out. The 'odd ones,' may become the great musicians, artists, designers or mathematicians, but may also have difficulty with learning to drive and we just have to find the correct key to their learning.

Cloze Comprehension reinforces the information by leaving gaps with only the minimum number of word prompts to be systematically filled in until the passage makes complete sense. Cross out every tenth word and read the passage again, then every fifth word and see if it can still be remembered and understood and so on, until all the information required has been learnt. When you are down to a blank sheet, you have remembered it all; with luck!

Common Sense is organising and structuring information by logical thought and building on previous experiences. e.g. if a triangle gives a 'warning:' a red circle gives 'orders or prohibition:' a blue circle gives 'positive instruction:' a rectangle gives 'information:' then it follows that a bike in a triangle is, 'Warning, Cycles Ahead,' a red circle is 'Prohibition, (you must not) No Cycles' and a blue circle is 'Instruction, (you must) Cycle Route'. From that one bit of information, the meanings of all the other similar signs can be extrapolated. It is transferable knowledge and most driving is about the ability to understand and transfer knowledge, not just to remember it. Unfortunately I often find experienced drivers who do not even understand the basics and so remain bewildered. A good example of this is the Priority Sign. Some drivers just stop at them irrespective of the sign and they tell me the reason for this is that they cannot work out which way the arrows are pointing. Of course they don't need to know, since the Red Circle indicates 'orders' and the Blue rectangle 'information.' It is just a matter of recognising if it is a red circle and then giving way. To get the message across, we need to simplify the basics and educate by public information programmes.

Memory Prompts use fridge magnets or put post-it notes where you are most likely to see them. Use a location such as the bedside cabinet, the fridge or a mirror. I remember having one extremely stressed lady who kept forgetting to be positive so I stuck a note to the dashboard, "I can pass this test" and she did. The examiner did not comment, but I know he took it in good spirit.

Many people including myself find the stopping distances difficult to remember and some panic at the thought of even trying to remember them. Firstly you don't have to remember them; you just have to select the correct ones from those given.

My method is to sort them out into **the norm, above the norm and below the norm.** I don't then need to remember anything, since I just reorganise the numbers. 50mph = 53 metres. That is the norm.

Above that speed will take considerable more braking, so it will be a plus figure; 60 mph = 73metres (60+) 70 mph = 96 metres (70+)
Below is minus the norm as it is easier to stop, so 40mph = 36metres (40-) & 30mph = 23metres (30-). We end with 23 -) 36 -) **53 norm)** 73+) 96+)

****

This memory support or mnemonic might be complete rubbish to anyone else, but as it works for me, it is therefore correct for me. Whatever works for you is also correct. It is up to you to sort out your own method. Don't necessarily rely on your instructor's methods and don't keep attempting the same thing if it is not working, as it just causes frustration. Use a different method and you will remember. We all have our own preferences and we can use any prompts which are applicable to us

Strategies for Learning the Practical

Practical Play. All the above senses can also be used effectively when learning the practical skills. Even if there are not any children around, most of us are near to a shop where toy cars can be purchased for a couple of pounds to assist this practical understanding. I bought a set of cars to demonstrate bay parking and also made one out of Lego with a steering wheel which actually steered the wheels, so I could show how the car performed when reversing and what effect the steering had on the wheels. (I could even change the hair of the doll to the colour of the driver's!) It is also possible to use matchboxes as cars, and table mats as corners to assist this visualisation.

Touching. I had the daughter of one elderly lady ask me to give lessons to her mother because she "drove by touch." I could well believe it, as every panel of the car had been bumped or scraped. Now I am not suggesting anyone uses her method, but a log as a guide in the garage, or ball dangling on a string, can assist positioning. It is necessary to feel the car working correctly so ask yourself, does it feel too bumpy; are the tyres inflated correctly; is it smooth etc?

Hearing. One can assist driving by listening to the car and the environment. When stopping at a junction, wind down the window and listen to the road sounds. If it is difficult to see, then it helps to be able to hear what is happening. The problem I find on some modern cars is that the radio on-off switches are too fiddly. In yesteryear they used to have a large button to hit, so I have marked the button on mine with tippex, to enable me to quickly silence it without having to put my glasses on. Some manufacturers are coming back to large hit-buttons, so they must also be realising that it is a safety issue.

Talking. Talk through what you are doing so that you get the correct sequence established in your brain via your ears. It is best if this is out aloud, but it does not have to be if it would be embarrassing. At a later stage of experience, talk through what you are seeing, rather than doing. This helps the brain to focus on what is required and prevents distraction.

Looking. If you do not understand what is happening, then get out of the car and watch others demonstrate the exercise. You will then be able to observe what the wheels are doing in relation to the steering wheel. Draw diagrams. One method I have used successfully is to put the back seats down and open the hatch, so the driver can actually see the road and does not need to rely on either judgement or guess work. Practise glancing, rather than staring at the mirrors in order to help make sense of the reverse image. As everything is back to front, it can require considerable practice, but the car does not have to be moving and the sequence can be practised in the quiet of your bedroom. Use long, short and middle distance vision to enable you to pick up the many driving clues around which help us to interpret and make sense of the driving environment.

Tasting and Smelling. Smell is an important safety issue, since we can smell the clutch when it is slipping or burning, as well as leaking hot antifreeze or other burning smells. It is very important when driving to be fully aware and to use all the senses, including smell and maybe even the pungent taste of fumes inhaled through the mouth.

****

These are just a few pointers to help your thinking to focus on what is right for you, but obviously the use of the computer and DVD has made some of these points easier to visualise, but computer use is only for those who can learn that way and many people still find the pen and paper and the old methods work best for them. Enjoy your study. That is the most important learning strategy. Don't let it overwhelm you or bore you. Remember inappropriate practice just causes failure and stress.

ii) MODE SWITCHES

One of the most important driving skills is to be able to prioritise and switch from one thing to another. This may seem obvious and for most people it is a natural ability, but for some it has to be taught, whilst for others it has to be recognised and focused on. It can be an innate problem and following stroke or brain injury it can be quite severe since the ability to switch appropriately may be lost or impaired. If a driver perseveres (Perseveration) on a train of thought, instead of switching, it can have serious implications which both the instructor and driver needs to be aware of. Listed below are a few processes, which in their own time and situation are perfectly acceptable to concentrate on, but it is not good when driving, as the priority and required skill is to be able to **SWITCH** between modes.

****

Driver Mode   This is when drivers need to concentrate on the road and consciously make sure that nothing else impedes on that total concentration, unless it is safe to do so. One of the biggest reasons for accidents amongst inexperienced drivers is distraction from other occupants of the car. This may be the distraction of mothers by young children and so we now have child seat legislation to minimise this distraction. There has sadly been a large increase in road deaths amongst the young, which is often caused by a group of teenagers in a car who drive without having had the experience to cope with the speed and the conditions and are then distracted by other occupants. Usually it is male drivers who are most at risk, since some drive beyond their limits and forget that disaster may be looming round the next corner. It is a sobering thought that many young men kill their girl friends by their driving. One of the jobs of an instructor is to be able to teach distraction skills and help the learner to respond appropriately. Some instructors just keep quiet and whilst that is appropriate some of the time, it is not a normal situation, causes uneasiness and therefore for most of the time is not a valid mode of teaching. Again there has to be a balance, but normal conditions of distraction must be taught. It is a skill to be learnt and practised.

****

Passenger Mode   "I like being a passenger, so I can see what is going on." This is a particular danger amongst some women who have spent years being driven around and when they have to drive, they find the habit of a lifetime difficult to break.

They can be in danger of running into the car ahead since they are looking at what is happening around them. Many times I have stopped and explained the need to concentrate on the road and if they want to look at things around them, then they need to pull over and stop. As soon as the car is rolling again the concentration can be distracted by the colour of a car, or the design of a building, or the fashion worn by a pedestrian, or what a shop is selling. The list is endless and concentration has to be taught and a conscious effort to learn to concentrate has also to be made. In my locality we have had drivers shoot over the cliffs and crash in car parks, so I deliberately take drivers into car parks overlooking our beautiful coastline and it is a salutary lesson to be learnt if they are distracted by the beautiful scenery **before** they have secured the car. Summer time can also present a problem of distraction to young (and old) men, but I will go no further down that pathway!

****

Pedestrian Mode   As a pedestrian one behaves very differently to how one should behave as a driver, but we need to check if the mind has switched appropriately to cater for these changes? A pedestrian may view a set of traffic lights differently to how one would as a driver and may give way on green and progress on red. One can also stop to look at things and get a better view or linger the gaze in order to comprehend more fully what is being observed. It is possible to change the mind or turn round, because something has caught their eye. There can also be pressures from passengers who distract or demand that the driver stops because they have seen something they want. These are luxuries not acceptable to be practised by drivers so they have to consciously keep switching. I am a great believer in the assistance given to the older driver by the passenger, but sometimes, if they are not drivers, they can forget the mode they should be in and revert to pedestrian mode and inadvertently distract.

****

Shopping Mode   I often get irritated at the way some people push their shopping trolley around the supermarket. They seem totally unaware of everyone else around them and blindly stop, or move off, or push the trolley through inappropriate gaps or block the aisles. It is obvious that many of them are not drivers, or if they are, they have left all their driving skills in the car park and become totally unaware of everything around them with their mind focused just on pushing the trolley. I do think shopping trolleys should be equipped with bells and have mirrors.

We cannot drive like that and I recommend that people who have difficulty in relating to other drivers actually practise by taking a trolley round a shop and learn to make the appropriate observation, as would be required from a driver on test. It is moderately safe and they should survive, except for a few bruised shins and they will then learn to be ready for the unexpected!

****

Home Mode   Most accidents happen within a mile of home, when owing to lack of concentration, the driver's mind flits to whether they have closed the front door or switched the cooker off or got their brief case. At the same time they are peering through the windscreen which may still be covered in mist as they have not bothered to clear it; the car is running cold and so the multi tasking causes distraction. As they enter the main stream of traffic they are ill prepared for any emergency which may occur. On returning to the 'security' of home, the same issues occur. 'What am I cooking for the meal?' 'Am I going to be late to collect the children from school?' 'Have I done everything I should have done?' The return home is one of the most dangerous times as the driver may forget to stop safely. On a number of times when instructing in the client's car, I have had to leap for the handbrake as the garage door has suddenly loomed closer and I have also had to assist when drivers (not being instructed) have gone through the garage doors or lost control in their driveways. As one approaches or leaves home, it is vital to learn to consciously switch to driver mode and if the mind requires space for the other non driving information, then stop and reconsider, but not try to do both at once.

****

Sleep Mode   Some people are owls, who find driving at night easy and others are larks, who get up early and are fresh at the beginning of the day. For the owls, who maybe have been up late at night, it is often impossible for them to drive safely for the first hour after getting up. I have taught youths for whom I would avoid arranging early morning lessons since nothing coordinates or sequences fluently at that early time. There is of course always the possibility of residual alcohol remaining in the body for many hours. Not only are they a liability on the road, but it does not do their confidence or learning experience any good and so it is a waste of their money and my time. I often wonder what they will be like when they have a full licence and have to drive to college. Hopefully by then, they will have learnt to be aware and cope safely.

Others find the night time difficult, but at that time it is easier to adjust their life style to safely compensate. Another aspect to this problem are those who take sleeping tablets or stay up late at night because they cannot sleep and then have to drive when they need to be asleep. Sleeping at the wheel is now being recognised as a very serious cause of accidents and driving with a lack of sleep has only recently been recognised to be just as dangerously antisocial as driving under the influence of alcohol or drugs.

****

Illness Mode   Many people still drive when ill or under the influence of alcohol or drugs and whether or not they are prescription drugs, they still have an effect and it is necessary to adapt safely to their possible effects. Some doctors say it is acceptable to drive with certain drugs, but there can be problems with muddled thought processes and sleepiness. If these tablets are mixed with even the slightest alcohol it can make for potential disaster and the possible effects need to be understood. I can remember the effects of antihistamine. To me the most obviously abused safety issue is smoking whilst driving. As a non smoker I have no idea how much it dulls the reactions, but certainly holding a fire in one hand must be potentially very distracting and dangerous and I can smell if someone is smoking even when they are two or three cars in front of me.

Many people drive with controlled medical conditions, but they must be proactively aware of the prodronal (early) sensations which give them an indication of when their condition may become more of a problem. All these must become conscious responses. Too often I hear people say "I never thought of the possible consequences". If drivers know they have problems, these need to be uppermost in their safety considerations and doctors should be more instructive in the effects of the interaction between various drugs, particularly when prescribing to older drivers who may get their dosage muddled. In the same way some people drive without glasses when they know they require them, which can even be for reasons of vanity, rather than just forgetfulness.

****

Talking Mode   This is our most common driving distraction and the most difficult to switch because it is something we naturally all do in so many different aspects of our day to day life. It therefore must become a conscious switch and not left to chance. Most people need to make eye contact when communicating and find talking when driving very difficult because they want to either lip read, eye read or face read.

It is quite instinctive for some drivers to turn to look at their passengers and yet very disconcerting and dangerous. My wife sometimes asks me what a person looks like and I have little idea, since I don't look at them when driving. I know them as personalities, because we converse a lot, but rarely do we actually look at each other. I am always aware of those who do not stop the conversation when approaching a hazard as it is something which then has to be taught. Other people stop the conversation quite instinctively and prioritise their thoughts on the road and this indicates a potentially safe driver.

We still get those drivers who see their car as their office and use their mobile phone when driving. It baffles me as to why it is necessary, unless it is to find directions or in the case of an emergency and it should then be possible to phone if the car is stationary. I think this is where the law has gone a stage too far in that the car has to be parked, but personally I would never drive with my mobile switched on and have never found I have missed an important call, so in my experience it has never been necessary. Messages can always wait until later when I am ready to give my full attention to them. I would suggest that people ask themselves at the end of each day, if there was any urgency to any of the calls made and if not, was it worth the risk to their lives and that of others. It is the distraction which is the greatest danger since the recipient of the phone conversation cannot see a developing situation and stop talking, in the same way that a passenger in the car would do.

****

Child Mode   If a child has been brought up in a strictly managed situation and have relied on the parents to do everything for them, they can have to learn how to make their own decision and after years of control it does not come easily. Some parents see this concern as a good thing, but are unaware of the long term consequences it can have on the driving development of their offspring. I have taken teenagers who have been unable to make their own decisions and at every junction have asked "Can I go?" They have even found it difficult to cross the road, because mum has always been with them or driven them in the car. These young people have to be taught to consciously switch and develop the confidence to make their own decisions and this can take a long time, because the instructor is detraining years of parental training and control, in order to then retrain. Sometimes, especially in the case of disability, they may never have developed the ability to make their own decisions or have actually lost the skill and the problem cannot be overcome to enable them to drive safely.

Parent Mode   I taught one lady who had never taken ownership of her driving because she was too scared to take risks, however calculated they were. When we analysed this response, it was because she had lost her mother at a tender age and she was determined to avoid risks to herself until her children were of a mature age. Out of concern for her own children, she had learnt not to drive appropriately, and had subconsciously chosen to avoid as many risks as possible. We had to develop her skill of recognising what was an acceptable, calculated risk, as well as recognising and being equipped to cope with the risk. Now the children were grown up, the pressure had gone and so within a short time success was achieved and she was able to travel to areas which she would previously have thought to be too risky. The subconscious pattern had to be broken.

****

Parking Mode   The ability to switch between parking and driving mode is so important and yet causes such irritation to other road users when instead of driving round the block and approaching from a different angle, they just stop the car for people to get out. The school run is one of the worst for this, with a total disregard for other road users or the danger presented to other children. The misuse of the blue badge scheme is another appalling scenario. Drivers park at dangerous junctions, because they erroneously think they can park anywhere. The driver using the scheme is sometimes not disabled, or maybe disabled but abusing the system by stopping for a non-disabled person to go and do the shopping. There seems to be a belief that the blue badge is for the car, rather than only for the individual who has been allocated the badge in order to allow them to personally get in and out of the car more easily and so assist their mobility.

****

Disco Party Mode   We have all heard the car blasting out inappropriate noise when in traffic jams and how the blood pressure begins to rise because of the intrusive noise, or worse still the beat which puts stress on the hearts of all around. If I was playing Beethoven at full blast whilst in a traffic jam, it would be just as inappropriate, because it is not to do with the choice of music, but rather the imposition of the noise on other road users and the distraction caused to the brain. I even know of a driver who crashed because of being distracted by being kissed whilst they were driving! The party had continued even when they had got into the car.

Distraction Mode   Any distraction can be a cause of danger, especially if it is not perceived as dangerous and it is not uncommon for drivers to have accidents whilst adjusting the radio, texting or using the Sat Nav. Learning appropriate focus and concentration is a skill which has to be taught and I believe it is just as important to be taught to recognise **when** it is safe to do things as **how** to do them. If one watches inexperienced drivers, they often change gear or may switch on their wipers when it is appropriate for the car, rather than when it is safe to do so. Awareness and avoidance of danger has to be taught and taking the hand off the wheel to change gear or looking in the mirror at an inappropriate time can prove to be just as dangerous as switching the radio or eating a biscuit. If we are not taught and do not exercise common sense in these matters, we cannot complain when we get a blanket imposition of the rules which are designed to protect us from ourselves and from each other.

****

Dress mode   We do not have such cold winters now, yet it is surprising how many drivers still dress in hats and coats which can get in the way of their movement and visual eye contact with other drivers. I remember one young lady often coming to lesson in most unsuitable and dangerous shoes. "But these are the shoes I will be wearing", was the comment. She had to be 'educated' to always carry a suitable pair of driving shoes. A few years ago, an important reason for road accidents in Japan was cited as the unsuitable footwear worn by women drivers. In the interest of safety it is necessary to drive in appropriate attire, to allow for free movement, unimpeded observations and to provide easy eye contact with other drivers. We still need to communicate with other drivers, even when we are in our secure bubbles. Sometimes just a nod and thank you is all that is needed to apologise for a mistake we may have inadvertently made. It makes everyone involved feel good.

****

Although this may seem to be an unusual section, I hope it has stimulated thought as to the wider responsibilities that drivers must have in addition to just demonstrating driving skills and to help illustrate and understand what other drivers may be thinking or doing in their own individual cars. Prediction and Awareness are huge areas of driving development which many younger people need to be taught. It is know as, Defensive Driving. Instructors may cover this area of learning, but what has happened to the Government information programmes which are supposed to educate us to really understand the road safety issues and so have an effect on how we drive? The Government also carries some responsibility. Please let us develop early understanding, rather than punishment when it is too late.

ERECTING a TENT

My wife and I love camping and over the years we have camped in many different countries. One of the real joys is to be able sit and watch other people. It can be a most informative 'people-watching' activity as many small communities live together within the larger community, yet bring with them their experiences and interactions of outside life whilst remaining individuals; in effect forming a microcosm of society in one small field. Just how a family erects a tent can indicate many things about the structure of their society. Let's look at a few of the learning styles and teaching styles used to erect a tent and then think about how the same characteristics are used when learning and teaching driving. Understanding people is a major factor in understanding how to drive safely and yet it is often ignored when teaching. It may seem a bit of an off-beat section to include here, but there is a wealth of analysis which corresponds to driving and learning and I leave you to make your own links. Can you identify your own driving instructor or learner?

****

1. Dominant Dad.   The children are instructed to sit in the car whilst dad erects the tent. That is his role; he knows exactly what to do and as long as he is not disturbed in the process, he efficiently succeeds in the shortest possible time, but woe-betide the child who wishes to help or ask questions! The result is that the child leaves everything to the alpha male, who always knows best, and they learn never to pluck up the courage to even try to help, however much they may wish to. They know they will never be good enough and whatever they do will be belittled, so they either sit watching and learning, but never actually taking part, or they just switch off in disinterest. His method cannot be questioned, because he is always right.

****

2. Spontaneous Girls. These are usually girls in a group who have made an unplanned emotional decision to go camping, but have no idea how to erect the tent they have borrowed and after struggling unsuccessfully, give up and let the older males, usually other dads or amorous lads on the site do it for them. Rather than learning how to do it, they stay put until another spontaneous desire overwhelms them and they enlist help again. They do not actually learn anything, but find that giggles and helplessness enable them to achieve their goal in other ways and they just cope with the minimum understanding.

3. The Instructing Father. Erecting a tent is a military 'Sound of Music' type activity. Every child has their own role which has to be done to perfection and with precision. It can be fun for those who learn that way, but often leads to fear if they get it wrong and as they are just part of the bigger plan, they never learn to do it for themselves. They always need the support of a team and cannot visualise the bigger picture, or work without being instructed. It is expected that the children will have understood, but they have no confidence to try for themselves.

****

4.The Nonchalant Youths As long as they are in a tent it does not matter how it is erected as long as they can fall to sleep, or play their guitars. It may collapse on them or blow away in the night, but that is something to be addressed if and when necessary. There is no planning, little care and everything is done on a needs-must basis. In a crisis they may cope, but their, 'could-not-care-less' attitude, ensures that mistakes are always likely to happen.

****

5. The Critical Father. "Your mum and I have done all the work putting up our tent and you cannot be bothered to put yours up. Well you can sleep in it as it is. You've made a mess of it. Look what you've done; you've pegged down the fly sheet before the tent. Get out of my way and I'll sort it out." I feel like getting involved, but prudence compels me to sit back and observe as the family relationships get fraught and the holiday, which should be so restful, is destroyed in anger and frustration. If only the child had been taught how to erect his tent beforehand, then the problem would not have occurred. The child did not want to make the mistakes or be shouted at, but he was too scared to try in case he got it wrong and when he did make a mistake he was shouted at. Whose fault is it anyway? For many children, planning has to be taught and the fear of disapproval inhibits their progress.

****

6. The Teaching Parent. "This is how you put up the tent; sort the poles into various sizes or colours, put them in this order, then one at a time lay them out like this and build a plan of the frame. You will be able to recognise if your plan is correct. Lay your pegs out in order and have your mallet near at hand. If you need to enlist help, then ask someone to hold the frame you have erected whilst you drape the tent over the frame and if it is not windy, you will then be able to secure it on your own.

If you feel you cannot remember all you have to do, then draw a plan to assist your memory, but do it before you need to". These MFI children have a flexible framework to work within, but they also have the freedom to develop according to their own natural personalities.

****

7. The well-meaning, but often ineffectual Mother who tries to keep the peace between the autocratic father and the rowing brood. How she wishes she was in a hotel in Benidorm and not in the mud and rain of the English country side with father wielding his macho club. This is not a holiday for her, but she tries to remain positive and keep the peace and pretend they are all enjoying it because father says they are. He organizes cricket and football on the field and they are usually louder than the rest of the campers put together and may have boozy parties at night to prove how much they are enjoying themselves. She is the mediator, who can see how the learner is becoming dispirited or angry and tries to ameliorate the situation because of the stress it is causing.

****

8. The Helping Parent. "I want to help daddy. Where do I put this piece?" This is the parent who allows the child to attempt to erect the tent under supervision, but gives tactical guidance when he is going wrong. The child is encouraged to develop and practise their own skills, but the stimulation comes from their internal interest and enjoyment. Although most of us come into the different categories at different times, I hope that both as a parent and a teacher, I primarily came into this category when teaching driving. I can remember my son at eighteen months amazing other 'watchers' on the camp site in Scotland, when he got all the colour-coded poles together and slotted them in their appropriate positions. He showed a great interest and satisfaction and enjoyed the corporate family activity. A couple of years later and his specific role and responsibility was to fill the water containers from the tap at the end of the field and carry them on his scooter. He felt good since his skills were both wanted and appreciated. Over the years he has developed many skills and can now turn his hand to anything practical or creative.

9. The Disaster.   I can remember camping in the Czech Republic and observing an Italian family try to park their caravan. The noise of the activity took over the whole camp as all the members tried to help. Every problem seemed to become a major issue and they seemed to accompany all their activity with loud involved shouting. They were all happy and admiring their corporate success, when suddenly the caravan set off on its own accord down the terraced hill side towards a steep and dangerous drop. In all the excitement, it had been forgotten that someone should have applied the parking brake. Everyone rushed forward and risking life and limb other fascinated watchers joined the chase and managed to avert the disaster a few feet before the edge. Shocked and embarrassed silence descended, as they realised that corporate activity is only safe if the person ultimately in charge takes responsibility. That is why driving instructors have dual controls. They are ultimately responsible.

****

Disaster 2.   I can remember camping in Northumberland and as the camp site was full we were directed into a farmer's field. It was very pleasant by the river until we observed our neighbours move their caravan. Husband was driving and his wife was directing him through the gate when an uneven rut caused the van to lean sharply to the right just as he was building up speed to pull onto the road. The gate post pinion caught and ripped a large hole in the side of the caravan. She stood there, hands clasping on her head and screamed "What did you do that for?" I vowed that if my wife ever made such a banal comment to me, it would be grounds for divorce. Of course she never has, but I often hear of similar comments made by ADIs to Learners who make mistakes. It is as if the instructor seems to think they meant to make the mistake. As they explain, they are mortified enough, without the instructor rubbing it in. They know they made an error and will make sure they never make it again. Now is not the time to discuss it, but maybe at a later date when they are calm and have recovered from the embarrassment, it can be fault analysed, to make sure it never happens again.

10. Uncoordinated or Disabled. There is no reason at all why uncoordinated or disabled people cannot camp or learn to drive. It just takes a little more planning, more time, more care and more understanding. I made sure my disabled cousin took part in most activities with which the able-bodied could cope. It is largely to do with personalities as to who will, or won't succeed and their interaction with those who are assisting them. The personalities covered above are still the overwhelming factors, but the disability is just an additional factor to be addressed. Some give-in, others fight, whilst others will even enjoy the challenge of having a problem to solve. What is not welcome is a patronizing attitude or over-fussiness. Some are scared to be creative or move outside their comfort zone and prefer to follow instructions, whilst others prefer to respond spontaneously to the random tangents which flood into their minds. Some are risk-takers who are driven by their creativity, but are unable to follow rules because they are distracted by a mass of tangential ideas. Others may have already been put off for life, because of the way they have been conditioned and then cannot work things out for themselves. They are frozen and cannot start to do anything unless told to or given permission. This can be the biggest problem for some of those who are disabled. It is not the disability, but the psychology which lies behind their conditioning.

****

People usually teach the way they learn, so if the learner is not achieving success, they should try and move on to someone they feel more comfortable with since many instructors do not mix and match their teaching styles. The instructor may have a natural bias, but out of knowledge, experience and insight may overcome their natural tendency and be able to teach in the way the client feels the most comfortable at learning. The upbringing and experiences of both the learner and the instructor are often key factors in the effectiveness of the learning. The Learner must also make sure the instructor is aware of how they learn, but the art of the teacher is to accommodate their learning style.

IV   HIDDEN COMMUNICATION

When we use the word communication, we usually think of the spoken word, but in many situations people do not communicate in that way. One main method of real communication is through body language, or by the hidden messages given out. The ADI needs to be able to understand that the messages not given verbally, may be much more relevant than the ones which are spoken.

Ask a question and the required answer will be given, but open a discussion and it is often surprising what is revealed. I have been amazed at the vehemence and anger which I have heard directed towards some other driving schools when we have passed them on the road. I have noticed the shakes and the sweats, which have proved to me that it has not been a slight disagreement with another ADI, but rather an extremely stressful situation which has been experienced and had far deeper implications on the learning difficulties we were now experiencing than I had at first imagined. I have observed drivers panic when 'trapped' in traffic, or even confronted with an open road, or pass into an area which triggers a memory.

When we go to the doctors, it is advisable to take a list of the issues we want to discuss because we can guarantee that we will walk away having discussed something trivial, rather than our real concerns which had of course been the purpose of the visit. The doctor was not embarrassed because he had seen it all before, but the patient was, because it was all new to them. Sometimes it is too difficult to bring ourselves to blurt out what is on our minds and it is left to the skill of the doctors to see beneath what we are actually trying to communicate.

The ADI is in many ways like the doctor in that they are in a one to one situation and the client is attempting to express what is wrong with them and what they feel and the ADI is in turn trying to identify what the problem is and trying to explain the diagnosis and then provide a prescription. We don't go to the doctor for him to proclaim the same as he told the last patient; this is wrong with you and this is what you must do; but instead we explain how we feel and expect to get relevant directed help and advice. If that help is not forthcoming or the wrong help is given, then we feel cheated, just as many learners do when they are told what they have to do even when they know it is not relevant to them and it is just the instructor's cold patter.

During my recent illness I have seen many doctors, but some of them have not had these interpersonal skills to make me seem important to them. My condition has been important to them, but that is a different issue since I needed to feel important and even when I have led the conversation in order to provide them with the opportunity to reveal more; because I actually want to know more; they have just kept to a clinical role. The result is that occasionally, I have come out feeling cheated that they have not listened to what I, as a person, have been trying to say and wanted to know. They gave me what they wanted to give me, which was not my agenda at all and seemed quite surprised when I asked for a video of my operation to enable me to understand what had actually been done to 'me'. That was obviously their domain and not mine and as expected my request was refused.

On the other hand I have an excellent GP, who although I rarely see him, when I do, he has the skill to identify my real concerns in a very short time which are the reason for my attending his surgery. It is not time consuming but rather a skill and the ones who have these skills are the doctors and driving instructors who will never be out of work, but it seems that under training and assessment only the clinical or driving skills are assessed, rather than the skills of communication. The real skill required is the ability to perceive what the client really wants to know, rather than what they say they want to know, or what the instructor wishes to impart, or what he has been told he should impart.

The ability to understand this hidden communication is very important when assessing how to develop the lesson and this understanding of the hidden messages needs to start from the very first lesson. As I have indicated above, quite often the spoken language will say one thing, but the body language will give quite a different message and the way these messages are read can go some way towards helping the instructor not only structure lessons, but also to tailor the way in which the teaching can be most effective. The learner not only needs to feel comfortable, but also stimulated and if one senses that boredom, fear or tiredness is setting in, then the activity needs to be changed. Observe, rather than blindly continue with the planned programme.

Learners have sometimes explained how exhausted they have felt on previous lessons because they have been doing the same thing time and time again and learning nothing, but the instructor has mistakenly thought they were offering good teaching through repetition, but missed the signals of despair and the sense of failure that had set in.

Unfortunately some instructors do this just before the test and the candidate then goes into the test feeling a failure before they have even begun the test. The art is to know when to abort the plan or the questioning, or change the conversation, or even go and get a cup of coffee. I timetable slots of time rather than a precise time and invoice for the actual time I give, so if the hidden messages I get are negative, I am able to terminate the lesson, but if they are positive and we are about to succeed at something we have previously failed at, then we will continue for a bit longer. This policy comes from my years of teaching maths and as soon as the bell rang we were expected to switch to English; just when we were about to make progress with the maths. When I set up my driving school I realised the same pattern of progressive learning was relevant and decided to try to read the hidden messages on that specific day and adapt the lesson to suit the learning needs of the client.

It is important to realise that a conversation with one client may be totally inappropriate with another, but they will not verbally inform the instructor, so the body language used is the only way one will be able to recognise this. When an instructor has got it wrong, I hear statements such as, "I was disgusted, but he thought I was one of the lads."

I am as guilty as the next one in not always reading the correct message, but I am aware of the problem and do try to check myself. We need to actively think about what they are saying and doing and whether it is indicating stress or insecurity or bravado or incompetence, because these manifestations are all giving the same message. Most people need their own personal space and feel uncomfortable in a small space and this is why I would not use a micro car for instruction, as it is important for the learner to feel comfortable and for the instructor to make them feel comfortable at all times.

****

Sometimes tact, sensitivity and understanding are required by the teacher. There is also need for honesty by the learner, since instructors cannot always be mind readers and many are not skilled at reading hidden communication, so please talk to your instructor about your worries. They are there to help you to both avoid and overcome any problems you may have. Too much silence is not a good thing as the focus is then directed towards the car, rather than the person. Too much talking can also be wrong, as some learners choose to chatter to detract from facing up to their real problems. All defence mechanisms exist to support perceived 'weaknesses' and must not be destroyed by challenging them in an insensitive manner. Only the individual concerned has the right to confront them, in order to learn how to cope without them.

V) <u>NO SHOUTING</u>

It may seem a strange chapter to have to write, but the biggest complaint that I hear from learners is, "he shouted at me." I can't think of any other business where people pay to be shouted at, yet it seems endemic amongst a considerable number of instructors and should be compared with 'Abuse in the Workplace.' I read one amusing but revealing comment, from a woman who had finally decided enough was enough as far as her instructor's shouting was concerned. It went something like this "I pay him to teach me. If I wanted to be shouted at, I can get that at home for free!"

The reasons for this shouting are many, but they have the common underlying theme of the unsuitability of the instructor, rather than the problems of the learner. I list a few possible reasons;

i)   - they have not been screened as to their suitability for the job.

ii)   - they have been inadequately and inappropriately trained, regulated and Check Tested.

iii)   - they are trying to fit the client into the DSA mould and when they don't fit, it causes both frustration and conflict.

iv)   - as 'instructors,' they expect to be obeyed and think that by shouting louder they will achieve their objective. It is the Sergeant Major Syndrome. "If only they listened to me, they would pass!"

v)   - even though it is the examiners who pass or fail candidates, they know that the DSA attributes failures to the ADIs and it is even considering publishing pass rates, they know they need to keep competitive and are frustrated at having to teach anyone who may be having difficulties.

vi)   - they are disillusioned, because they are floundering and not making the income they were promised by the misleading advertising, which took them into training in the first place,

vii)   - they feel angry and stupid that they did not research the business and think about the small print,   even though they are reasonably intelligent, but now they feel they have been conned.

viii) -they bring personal problems to work, which are often of a financial   nature.

ix)   - they are exhausted, by having to work long hours to pay the franchise fee and have no time for themselves or their family.

x)   - they believe that shouting will get the message through, because that was their learning experience and they have not been taught any different methods.

xi)   - they are Potential Driving Instructors and, unknown to their clients, they are about to fail their final instructional examinations and are suffering the stress of having to give up instructing.

xii)   -they do not understand the needs of their clients, nor the way they learn and are skill-orientated instead of being-person directed.

xiii)   -they are over- protective about any potential damage to their precious car, which instead of being regarding as a workhorse, is only seen as a huge personal investment.

****

One only has to look through Yellow Pages to find ADIs advertising, 'No shouting guaranteed'. It is necessary to read between the lines, as this of course could also mean, 'I am a boring instructor who shows no emotion or enthusiasm', but it is so sad to have to advertise 'patient and professional' as attributes, rather than expectations. It is like saying 'I will not beat my wife'. Occasionally, when I have had to raise my voice or grab the wheel I have apologised and the response on one occasion was. "You have never shouted at me, but you have been firm and made me focus because I need to be pushed." I have decided that it is attitude which matters and how the relationship is perceived, that can either make it an acceptable raising of the voice, or alternatively turn it into an aggressive shout. In case of danger or enforcement, then it is acceptable to raise one's voice, as one would do in real life and of course this would be understood and accepted by the learner without any complaints.

I am sure many of us have watched some of the appalling television shows about driving. I deliberately use the word 'show,' because they never seem to be able to make a serious programme about learning to drive. It always has to have the aim to embarrass the learners, or to portray unrealistic scenarios and driving seems to be a comedy to the programme makers, but to the clients it is a very serious issue. In these shows, we have all watched the unacceptable forms of 'abuse' which have taken place when the instructor has either been instructing totally inappropriately, or shouting, or completely not understanding how the learner should be learning. The worst aspect is that most of these are condoned by the DSA and they even allow the use of the DSA examiners and Test Centres.

One programme I protested about was when an older lady was being forced to drive a manual car, which regularly contributed to her failures. She obviously could not cope and needed an automatic to remove her stress and help her succeed, but this would not have been good television. My oldest first time pass was seventy-six when she completed her Pass Plus Course, but of course it was on an automatic and would have shown real learning in a safe environment, rather than the 'fun' of extreme stress. I suppose creating driving stress for television is rather like watching bear bating or dog fighting, but for some instructors there seems to be a total lack of understanding of stress and how to prevent it. Another programme which vividly remains in my mind was when the instructor shouted, "Do it my way" and then when he got the belligerent response his actions demanded, he added sarcastically, "Alright do it your way and get it wrong." I can remember one woman saying how her instructor shouted "Listen to me. If you listened to me you would get it right." and then she added; "he did not seem to realize that he was the problem and he made me frightened and that was why I made mistakes."

Another described her lesson, "he still wasn't happy so I was called a stupid **** and told I was ****ing terrible. This destroyed my confidence early in the lesson and I still had another hour and a half to go; he then proceeded to belittle me on everything, until I was doubting even my most basic driving skills; he wasn't even letting me make the mistakes, just grabbing the wheel before I had a chance to make a mistake; in the end he was even using the dual control pedals in anticipation of me not braking quickly enough or raising the clutch too quickly. On the drive home, he lit a fag and poured some coffee from his flask and announced, "I don't think you will ever pass!" I felt like crying there and then."

One came sobbing in despair on the phone to me and poured out her troubles, "He just lost the plot and lost it with me. I am so frightened. I am already nervous and bereaved with no confidence and he has made me lose it all now. It's all gone. He just shouted at me and I froze. I don't know whether to bother anymore. I don't know if it is worth doing. My error was in not coming to you in the first place and it turned into a nightmare. Two hour lessons, two hours of dread and fear. I ended up locking myself in my house and hid behind the settee when he called. I cried all the time". She was a bright, competent lady with no problems at all, who went on to pass first time after only a few lessons and it changed her life. There was no need to shout. There never is.

What is wrong with some driving instructors that make people talk with such vitriol about them? It is not the job of one ADI to have to pick up the pieces of a learner whom another instructor has broken. They should not be teaching that way in the first place and so make people lose their confidence. Another of my clients explained, "Even today his abuse is so vivid, that I could take you to every road and every roundabout where he shouted at me and terrorised me. Why did I as a mature woman pay thousands of pounds to be sworn at for so long? Why could I not break the pattern? I tried to explain nicely that I did not appreciate it, but he took no notice."

****

If you have got problems, first talk to your instructor and tell them how you feel and if they don't change, then you change instructor. Don't accept the 'battered wife syndrome' and stay with them out of fear. Use your feet, because if they are creating your problems, or making your situation worse, it will cost you more money and stress. I had one learner who said, "He 'terrorised' me. 'He sucked my confidence dry'. 'He was a leech, but you gave me back my confidence." It should not be so and as an industry we must stop both this abuse and the causes of this abuse.

I could write a whole book on similar examples and if there is not a change in ADI selection and training, then I may have to do just that. The DSA seem content to look at the wrong issues, because if they look at the real ones which concern attitudes towards people, it may illuminate how fundamentally wrong their prescribed system is for some learners.

Section 5 Approved Driving Instructors

i)   What do you do?

ii) Do the Maths.

iii) My Staffroom.

iv) Looking Forward

v)   Conclusion

i) WHAT DO YOU DO?

I was so excited when I qualified as an ADI, and as it was something I had always wanted to do I needed to tell everyone. It was almost as good as when as a student I became a bus driver. I put my certificate on my bedside cabinet, so when I woke in the night I knew it was not a dream. Personally, it meant far more to me than qualifying as a teacher. That was something I did to put bread on the table. This was something I did for myself, because I wanted to do it. Isn't it interesting how when we first meet someone we always feel the need to ask about status. What do you do? So we think up all sorts of fancy names to put a better spin on our work to make it more acceptable to others. It is the John Cleese/Two Ronnies' sketch. 'I know my place' and until we have established our place in the group we actually find it difficult to communicate. It is not who we are, or what we think, but what we do, that seems to indicate our status and determines whether we should look up or down.

It was always a family joke, that if I had told my future mother-in-law that I was a bus driver or driving instructor, she would have thought, "I have given my daughter all that education, she could do better," but if I said I am a Teacher, the conversation attained a higher level than if I said I was a Driving Instructor. Why is this, when essentially I am still doing the same job? If I say I am a learning facilitator or mentor, then that is regarded as jargon and a conversation stopper; so I have always just said, "I am a teacher." "What do you teach?" is the follow up question, but when I answer, "people," I get a pitying look and an exasperated sigh, followed by, "no what subject do you teach?" "Well I have never taught a subject, honestly, I have always taught people."

In my previous career, when I used to say "reading", that was also a conversation stopper since anyone, even parents, can teach reading, that is not a subject. Now I say "driving," that is also not regarded as a subject and something which anyone, even parents, can teach. Apparently you do not need any real skills to teach either reading or driving! So I add, "I am a Specialist Driving Instructor." "I have never heard of one of those; what do you specialise in?" and so the conversation develops. In actual fact, there is officially no such thing as a Specialist Driving Instructor, because according to the DSA we are all the same, but I can legitimately say I am a Specialist Teacher- of driving. I have always been a teacher specialising in helping students how to learn whatever they are studying and at present that concerns people who find driving difficult.

To some people the word teaching, conjures up lecturing or imparting knowledge, whereas to others it is a person who develops learning. I just know that I am not an Instructor, never have been and would never wish to be, although officially that is how my work is described. I certainly am not a Trainer as they train animals to respond as the master wishes. Learning- facilitator is actually a better term, as it does not only incorporate instruction and teaching, but primarily covers helping people to learn in their own particular ways. As the term still seems to be pretentious I stick with teaching, because I'm an educator rather than an instructor and 'the man in the street' has some understanding of the term.

I soon realised that not everyone shared my enthusiasm for the work and the introductory question on the phone from those asking for lessons was often, "What do you charge?" At first I found there was no kudos and the status that society viewed driving instructors was indicated by the low level of income one could get from the job and that was the crux of the problem. It was a job and not a career and certainly it was not for many the passion that it was for me. Some instructors came into it because they just thought it was an easy job and charged the lowest rate they could survive on and provided a corresponding level of service. My excitement of the work soon began to cloud as I met instructors who did not see it as their job to understand how people learnt. They just wanted to tell people what to do and had no real interest or understanding of people and their specific needs. Some of their conversations horrified me.

As in all professions, some had been in the job for too long and gone stale and had not developed their professionalism, whilst others were unsuitable, or too inexperienced and ill trained to see the real issues and I soon began to realise why the general public viewed ADIs in such a way and why the Government held us in such low esteem. I listened to an older instructor explaining that he had found the job useful, since he did not require any academic qualifications and could just keep his hand in without learning anything new. No doubt he had had years of experience on which he had built his skills and probably had forgotten just how much he had actually learnt in the process, but it seemed to belie the numerous and complex skills that are necessary to be a successful teacher of driving and I felt that comments such as his undermined the profession. I also think he probably undervalued what he had learnt and had to offer through his experience and many drivers would have appreciated all he had taught them, but society seems to undervalue instructors with experience, especially those who think for themselves.

There are many brilliant driving instructors and even if we do not agree with each other, we feel keen to share ideas and learn from each other's experiences. Unfortunately, because of the poor, isolated ones, the Government, through the DSA, seems determined to destroy the flexibility of the good instructors, just as they did with the good teachers when they imposed the National Curriculum. They seem intent on controlling the methods of instruction, instead of developing a wide spectrum of concepts and working practices to meet the personal needs of the clients. Appropriate regulation is necessary, but it can become suffocating to new ideas when it is inapplicable and applied like a blanket, especially when free market forces are already there to regulate the market place.

When I taught Careers in schools in the 70s, we used a programme with set questions to ask our students and according to their responses, it recommended a suitable career. The careers selected for the male students with low academic achievement, but with a practical aptitude and an interest in cars, were always 'mechanic' and 'driving instructor.' A decade ago when I was teaching in the Independent School, I tried to suggest to the hierarchy the potential career opportunities that there could be in the driving industry and that maybe we could offer driver education as an academic subject. The suggestion was belittled, because it was certainly not regarded as a career for their students to consider and I was asked if I could imagine the parents accepting 'Driver Education' in the School's Prospectus. But, things are changing and it is now possible to get a Masters degree and a Doctorate and there is now a corresponding University Chair in Driver Education. The DSA needs to recognise that it is into a new era of driver education and it is not now dealing with the non-academic instructors of yesteryear, who could only work satisfactorily if under its control and instructing to a set system. Whether it is recognised or not many of us are already professionals.

It is becoming a profession for others, but the financial status is still not there for the majority and the career insecurity resulting from the uncapped DSA Register is causing too many inexperienced ADIs to come into, and then rapidly leave the profession, so adding to its instability. It is not only the fault of the DSA, but also some affluent parents who regard learning how to play a musical instrument or golf lessons, or attending a gym or going on exotic holidays, as more important than paying for enough potentially life saving driving lessons.

Other parents just cannot afford what is necessary to provide for the safety of their children and some do not understand that things have radically changed from when they learnt to drive. When the overheads of a driving school are so high and the driving instructor may be only taking home the equivalent of a supermarket shelf stacker, is it any wonder that some instructors are forced to undervalue their skills and work to the level of income they receive?

The basic skills listed on my school careers programme are very different from the ones I have come to realise are the essential ones to becoming a successful driving instructor. Every day I am presented with a new challenge because I am dealing with people and not machines and people are unpredictable. The instructor needs a genuine interest in the clients as people, because the learners can easily sense whether or not the Instructor is really interested. It soon becomes obvious if they are preoccupied with the mechanics of the business and their income or whether they are going to be able to earn enough that week to be able to pay for the petrol and the fees for the car, let alone the mortgage.

What skills and knowledge base are required ?

i)   Educational Psychology, to understand how people learn and the problems they may have.
ii)   Teaching, Tutoring, Mentoring, to effectively impart knowledge.
iii)   Maturity, having had many life experiences to fall back on.
iv)   Science, to explain the effects of physical forces and the handling of the car.
v)   Orientation, with an ability to map read and find the way around.
vi)   Awareness, of potential hazards and an innate ability to respond accordingly without panic.
vii)   Lateral thinking and problem solver, so as to be able to see the hidden message.
viii) Mechanic, with the ability to explain the basic function of cars.
ix)   Communication, with an ability to give clear instructions.
x)   Ability to cope with external frustration outside of one's control.
xi)   Bereavement Counselling and how loss and preoccupation affects learning.
xii)   Social Work and an understanding of how personal problems affect learning.

xiii) Reasonably good driving skills, but not that important.

xiv) Listening and the ability to pick up hidden as well as spoken communication.

xv) An ability to be empathetic and sensitive.

xvi) To be a good conversationalist and able to enter into the world of the client.

xvii) Knowledge of medical issues to understand the effects of illness, pain, disability and medication.

xviii) Diplomatic, so as to know when to refrain and when to offer an opportunity to talk openly.

xix) Business Management, so as to know the best way to manage finances and marketing.

xx) Organisational, so as to be able to manage the day to day diary effectively.

xxi) Environmental, with an understanding of Eco Driving and green fuels.

xxii) Experience in Understanding Stress and Psychological Problems.

xxiii) Understanding and sensitivity towards different cultures and races.

xxiv) Ability to tutor non academics and foreign language students with the Theory

xxv) Ability to make learning interesting.

****

In the interests of road safety, it is essential that we raise the status of the profession, but it seems that the DSA constantly belittles driving instructors by undervaluing their work and presenting them with more controls and hoops to jump through. If I consider the personal frustrations I have encountered through DSA incompetence towards my clients and multiply that throughout the country, it is obvious that we need valid support and recognition for the work we do. The individual ADIs struggle to be efficient, but as we labour under a Government monopoly we are not free to take our custom elsewhere and do not have the freedom we need to raise the status of our profession. It sometimes feels as if we have a mill stone weighing down our profession and our professionalism and sadly that is our own governing body.

DO THE MATHS

Sometimes I am approached by drivers asking how they can become Driving Instructors, but when I ask them as to their motives for wanting to be an instructor very few start with what they can bring to the business, but rather how driving instruction will fit into their lives. I then ask what gave them an interest in instruction and they nearly always quote some advert offering great riches. This is followed by stating their driving and mechanical abilities. Of course they are looking at the wrong things, so I may continue by asking them if they have thought through why there are so many training companies offering these riches, rather than them actually making their money by teaching all those learners who want to drive. It soon becomes obvious that there is no demand for most of these new instructors, but the courses are being provided because there are now very few teenagers actually wanting to learn to drive and as business is business, more instructor-training is taking place. The reasons for this dearth of learners are quite clear;

i)   a drop in the birth rate:
ii)   a lack of money, because good lessons are expensive:
iii) the increased school pressures of continual assessment studies, rather than the previous system of only having exams at the end of Year 13, which used to leave plenty of time for driving lessons:
iv)   fees for university, which need to be worked and saved for:
v)   a lack of parking at universities:
vi)   huge insurance costs for the under 25s:
vii) the increased difficulty of the Theory Test, which is preventing access for the less academic who actually need to drive:
viii) the increased difficulty of the Practical Test and the likelihood of failure.

****

Then we come to the essential questions I ask. What can they bring to the business? What is their teaching ability and experience like? Have they the skills of communication? Have they the ability to listen as well as to instruct? At last they are beginning to think, rather than just hope. I heard one Driving Instructor liken Instructor Training to the X factor, whereby there are plenty of wannabes who believe they can do the job, but on the show there is Simon Cowell to give them a reality check and send them on their way.

They may be excellent karaoke singers when in the pub, but it is a different world out there and there is no one to give PDIs that reality check, before they part with their large sums of money. Unfortunately many get hooked on the 'double glazing' salesman patter, who ply them with the wonders of the job until they cannot say no and so they sign the cheque for a few thousand pounds without really reading the small print or understanding the issues. Some of the questions to be asked are.

i) Can you afford the time and cost of training which could be 2 years?

ii) Can you afford to work long hours for very little income, when considering that your learner with no overheads, could be taking home more money working at the supermarket, but still think you are expensive compared to the trainee or desperate new instructor down the road.?

iii) Can you put up with the interference of the DSA in your self employed business, who will also tell you how you should teach your learners, even if you know it to be wrong?

iv) Can you accept the 'failure,' or as I would call it the 'arrested development' of the learners whom you have struggled hard to teach and who have made such good progress under your tuition?

v) Can you cope with test cancellations, when you have carefully mentored your learner towards reaching the required standard for a set date and then find you may have to wait weeks before having their 'induced' failure logged against your name as your responsibility?

vi) Are you a competent business person, or would you find it less stressful to stack shelves at Tescos?

vii) Do you realise that to pay your overheads and franchise fee, you may have to work for the first three days of every week of the year, without any actual income?

viii) Are you aware of the large amount of dead time between lessons, including travel and waiting time to be budgeted and paid for?

ix) Are you prepared for the unreliability of the public? (I hear about this, but fortunately unnecessary cancellations are not something I have experienced.)

x) Are you aware that it is the clients and their tests, which will determine if, or when, you get any time off?

xi) Are you aware that there are close on 100,000 trainees and instructors offering some form of instruction and then ask if there can be enough work for all of them?

xii)   Have you got someone else to help pay your bills, or do you have a private income or pension to help you survive the lean times, during holidays or Christmastime, when your learners may choose to spend their money elsewhere?

****

Now the reason I am covering this here is that, if an instructor is disillusioned, feels tricked, is stressed because they are about to fail their instruction exams, cannot find enough money for the petrol, is exhausted by the hours they are having to work; then the learner is being short changed and the whole profession is being dragged down. Much of the 'short fuse,' poor instruction comes from unhappy instructors who are on edge and it becomes a cycle of despair. The career pathway for some of these struggling instructors is to then do a month's course to try to become examiners. I am not referring to those experienced career examiners whom we all respect, but those who see being an examiner as a last gasp effort to make something out of their large investment.

They are pushed into it because they have little option to make ends meet and have become desperate and when the test waiting times get too long for the Charter Mark conditions the DSA recruits more sessional examiners so this can be a way out. Personally I would find being an examiner quite soul destroying, but then again we are all different and I know some enjoy it; are content, get satisfaction from their work and are very good at their job. I have great respect for those examiners with whom I have worked over many years. It has been a partnership of professionals.

If after all this, you feel you are still inspired by all you have read here, then you will probably make a good instructor. It is a great job, but come into it with your eyes wide open and you will not be disappointed. You will have the power to change people's lives and that means everything. For me it is the best job I have ever done, but my motive was how to fill the need that I had identified. In those two decades the job has changed greatly for the worse, although the need I saw then is growing even greater and there are tremendously exciting challenges for anyone who has the courage to embrace them.

****

I would say to any would-be ADI, if you can supply the expertise to meet a Specific Need and have the financial resources to remain solvent until you have developed your business, then we need you in the profession, but to adapt the famous quotation, 'think not what driving instruction can do for you, but rather what you can bring to driving instruction.'

iii)   MY STAFFROOM

I am sure you know where this is for you. It is your sanctuary; the place where you collapse or let off steam when you have had a bad day at the office; or you have just taken year eleven who do not seem to understand what you are talking about, nor understand the urgency of their exams; or you have had a stroppy patient on the ward who has been anything but patient; or you have had to pretend that 'the customer is always right,' when you know they are clearly wrong.

A Driving Instructor does not have one of these staffrooms so it is essential to create a place which provides the same function, otherwise one can become out of touch, ill informed or lonely. When I first entered the profession I became a member of the Driving Instructors' Association, which through their magazine kept me informed of the issues concerning our business. I regularly write for the magazine 'Driving Instructor' and have both attended and spoken at the DIA conferences. I became a committee member of my local group at the Bournemouth and District Driving Instructors' Association, (BDDI) which both keeps me informed of what is happening locally and also provides me with an input into local issues. I write regularly for the 'ADI News', which is a magazine providing a wide view of the issues affecting our work and also for our Union Magazine, 'The Way Forward,' as well as writing for my local district magazines on various driving issues which are of interest, or of concern to our local community.

Rather late in the day I subscribed to broadband and my whole support chain was transformed with my membership of the Driving Instructors' Democratic Union, (DIDU) which is a growing influential group of experienced and thinking driving instructors who want what is best for our business and have the professionalism, experience and intellect to develop our industry for the benefit of both the clients and the instructors. Having been someone who has never taken strike action I was a little concerned as to the historical connotations of the word Union, but I can assure anyone reading this that it is just a united and equal group of unpaid individual instructors that I am proud to be part of.

There will be some members, maybe many, who do not agree with what I have written in this book, but I know they will defend my right to express what I think and will in a reasoned and reasonable way, look at the issues raised.

They will discuss them without malice and sift what may be valuable to them in their day to day work and maybe argue about the others. It is the individual ideas and experiences within our group which make us so united and rather than become a homogenous mass, we have instead retained our individualities. We are united in our aim to improve the lot of all those concerned in our industry and to use all our powers to influence the prevention of death and injury on our roads especially to our young people and to make our business both successful and accountable.

It is really great to be able to receive the support of other instructors, many of whom I have never met, but I know we can nevertheless be serious, funny, share problems, gain first hand up to date information and even at times be stupid and let off steam, just as one would do in a staff room. We are not passive members, but an active voluntary group that has become a valuable tool in the support of each other and of driving instructors in general and I look forward with interest to its continuing influence on the future of driving instruction. The birth of the union numbered the days of the passive instructors, in that we decided that never again would we be steamrolled through ignorance of the facts which concerned our industry.

Another aspect of keeping in contact and understanding the business, is through maintaining wider contact with other drivers throughout the country who may just be beginning to learn, or be experienced and want to share their experiences; they may be examiners, instructors or trainees, or just the general public who want to share their skills and knowledge with others. I do this primarily through my contact with the 2Pass Forum and whilst I have disagreed and argued with many members, I regard them as a family where we can always bounce back and share our experiences and thoughts and gain knowledge and information from each other, whilst helping new members along the way. As contributors become successful, there are always some who are leaving, but then there are others who are joining to replace them. The feedback I get on the Special Needs advice I give is very positive and appreciative and I have made some really good friends and heard of some amazing successes.

There are other forums I use such as Driver Training Today, but one could spend all one's time on the net and never get round to actually teaching, which of course is my principal goal. There are other groups who provide 'Staff Room' services to driving instructors, such as Motor Schools Association, The Federation or UKDI Confederation and I have contact with many instructors who are members of these and of other associations, but it has not been the way I have been led and my reason for writing this is to encourage people to get involved with whatever suits them best and become informed and not be isolated or lonely. The ignorance of many ADIs as to what is happening and what is planned for our industry amazes me. How are we going to make our voices heard whilst there is still time for action, if we do not know about the issues, before they become 'fait accompli'?

My plea to instructors and learners alike is get into your Staff Room and get involved and informed, rather than complain about things when they are imposed and it is then too late. Like many other instructors I was one who asked the DSA for the opportunity to be able to analyse the Hazard Perception Test (HPT) and Multiple Choice Questions (MCQ) in order to help our learners and to enable our teaching to be more effective. Instead we had a test imposed which achieved nothing and has been of no benefit to our clients and statistics would indicate of no benefit to Road Safety. It seems that the DSA does not listen to the ideas of those who matter, but just grabs onto anything that comes its way and then misappropriates it and if it is not working, it then makes it even harder. There are major Disability Discrimination issues to be addressed regarding the Theory Test which cannot be achieved in isolation, but together we will provide for those academically less fortunate who wish to drive legally.

I have chosen to go on numerous valuable educational courses during my career and a few courses since becoming an instructor, but we must demand 'relevant' Continual Professional Development (CPD) and the right for us to decide what is correct for our clients and for us personally, rather than having some irrelevance imposed. Can you imagine any other educational establishment where the examiners control the exams, the teachers, the syllabus, the results, the exam papers and the way the teachers achieve the exam results?

****

I think our 'staff rooms' will now make sure we are not misled in the same way again and our successes will be passed on to our clients in the form of improved services. Remaining disparate individuals will only leave us in the dark ages, so come and join us, since together we can make a change for the better.

LOOKING FORWARD

To summarise the fundamental issues facing driving instruction in the immediate future one has to recognise that, even though instructors are self employed, they are still governed by the DSA and it is the DSA which controls how instructors teach. Many of us have realised from experience that the methods demanded are not the best ways of achieving competence or safety from our students. We have therefore chosen to vary our practice to suit the needs of our clients. This is partly self preservation, since instructors know that if they taught how they were trained to instruct then many learners would choose to go to those teachers who offered something different and so they would soon be out of work. But for others, it is a deep belief that we should try to understand and meet the needs of our learners. There are some instructors, especially those recently trained, who believe that what they have been told is the only way and many clients remain with them because they are misguided in thinking this is the way they have to learn, even though they may know that it is not being successful for them. If it is not working, then there is a need to break the mould and start again and this is as true for the DSA as it is for the learner.

The learner needs to understand why it is so difficult and expensive to learn to drive and they must first look at the structure of the DSA and realise it has no motive to actually get people to succeed, because it is driven by failure and it is only through client failure, that it is financially successful. Most businesses are judged by their success and with success come the rewards, but the DSA works the opposite way round. When cornered, it can of course always say it is to do with road safety and the more KSIs (Killed Seriously Injured) there are, the more it feels justified in enforcing its methods of failure. If we analyse the road safety implemented by the DSA it would be difficult to find any real improvements, because it will just inspect its own limited boxes, instead of seeing the whole picture. Even if we consider the recent official statistics, there has been very little improvement overall and the small improvement observed, has largely been as a result of the introduction of air bags, safety cages, ABS/ESP, improved road engineering and advances in paramedic care.

We must consider the wider picture of increasing social deprivation and anti social behaviour exacerbated by this DSA control of licences. This is conveniently being ignored by those who would choose to restrict, rather than to educate. There are even some who advocate the withdrawal of licences as a punishment for unrelated matters.

I wonder if they also plan to withdraw A levels or degrees for white collar fraud and by removing those livelihoods also condemn them to the Social Needs Register.

The majority of instructors are struggling to make ends meet, but some are a real success and the reason for this may be that they have the courage and experience to be different and refuse to do what the DSA in its ignorance wants. Other instructors are suffering because of the unreasonable demands of the DSA, which seems not to be able to understand even the basics of learning and therefore of teaching and who compiles statistics which measure the wrong factors. The fall in the level of instructor's income is resulting in good experienced teachers leaving the profession, whilst at the same time boosting the flow of new applicants, many of whom are at first likely to be inadequate teachers. These are welcomed, since they pay their fees and may be controlled into becoming 'good instructors'. Unfortunately very few of these succeed, but there are always those waiting to being enticed by promises of great riches, so it is again another policy based on DSA income, whilst seriously affecting safety on our roads.

In the public interest we need to retain these experienced teachers, rather than to develop the new puppet instructors, when statistically most of them are destined to become failures. Misleading advertising should be banned and there needs to be a halt to this spiral of failure by capping further entry to the register, until the disastrous consequences of allowing unlimited numbers of inexperienced trainee instructors to flood the market, are really thought through. Those who apply to be instructors should be carefully selected as to their teaching suitability and the content and emphasis of the training courses need a complete rethink as to what the aims really should be. The courses must have a greater educational bias than the present instructional ones which lead to continual failure.

The idea that drivers can become examiners after only four weeks training is quite absurd. I wonder how many of the real issues I have been covering here are even discussed in either instructor or examiner training and how many of them are considered in depth. Does that therefore imply that all I have written here is pointless, or that instructors and examiners are being wrongly trained with the wrong emphasis? I believe the instruction syllabus is so sadly restrictive, that it results in candidates being inappropriately taught and ill prepared for driving on today's roads. This then has negative implications on road safety and could be contributing to some of the tragic accidents that our young people are involved in.

There needs to be a change in the balance of the training of instructors and examiners from skill training, to communication training and they need to learn to communicate at the level of the learner and understand how people think, learn and function; i.e. the Psychology of Driving. It may be even counter productive to be a highly trained driver, in that they can come to believe that they are experts and wish to show off their expertise, when they are actually experts in the wrong thing and need to be experts in understanding failure, rather than success. Maybe we require more instructors who have struggled, but actually understand why they have struggled and what they have learnt from it.

Another concern is that the DSA could become hand in glove with big business and this would be very detrimental to road safety. I can see the day not too far off, when the independent instructors, with independent ideas are forced off the roads by the present system and only big business remains to instruct in the DSA way and so enable them to make money for each other, without any checks. Just as teachers in education need to distance themselves from big business, so also ADIs need to remain free and independent thinkers; free to be able to develop ideas and free to offer the level of service to their clients which they have become successful at providing.

I find it sad that my business of Road Safety can even be reduced to satirical comedy depicting the pointless insistence on inappropriate systems and also that many learners are giving up the chance of learning to drive, because they feel they are being conned by what is being inappropriately expected of them. The many television 'shows' about driving, which are supported by the DSA, have done nothing to enhance the status of our profession and the driving industry has become a laughing stock: a very sad laughing stock, because it is contributing to wasted lives, hugely wasted resources and opportunities, as well as adding to great social hardship. I am all for 'getting on your bike' and using public transport, but I do believe most people should have the social skills to drive, in order to enrich and fulfil their lives. Most of us do not need large cars for daily use, so the immediate future of the micro car for towns and the larger hire cars for the family holiday is almost upon us, but we all still need to be able to drive and become experienced at driving. It does not mean more cars on the road, but a more efficient use of private cars which working together with public transport can produce a smaller carbon footprint. I totally concur with the Minister of Transport's statement, "We must provide people with the skills to make their own choices."

The most absurd system imposed on experienced instructors is 'The Check Test'. This is when the DSA sends examiners, often with inadequate training or experience, to Grade highly skilled teachers in the way they should be instructing; not according to the needs of the client, but according to an impersonal, theoretical, training book. It must be highly embarrassing for these examiners who have no freedom to evaluate anything outside of the set boxes and who must be acutely aware of their own inadequate knowledge as to the work the instructor undertakes and the reasons for the decisions that are made. If it was war time, where it was necessary to regulate and keep the troops in order, then it may still have some relevance, but I can't imagine any other so called profession, being prepared to put up with such a divisive system of control, especially when any discussion is only allowed, 'after' the grade has been allotted.

I apologise for coming back to this point again, but it really is most insulting and the height of regressive thinking by Civil Servants acting way above their ability, understanding, training, or status. It is possible for instructors to get away with inadequate instruction, malpractice and even illegal practices, but as long as they can perform role play for one hour, then they will be regarded as a "fit" person to instruct according to the set system. On the other hand, excellent instructors can be demoted for providing a personal service to their clients. Excuse my vitriol, but it is a completely mad and outdated system which needs at once to be radically revised. The efforts of the Supervising Examiners could then be redirected to where they will actually have some influence in reducing the KSIs and in raising standards and the expectations of the many learners and instructors who suffer under the present antiquated system of control.

It is quite unbelievable that instructors are not part of a Professional Assessment, where the ADI has an equal professional input together with experts in their field of expertise, which is followed by discussions regarding relevant CPD (Continual Professional Development) to improve their individual skills. In no way am I implying that instructors with high grades are poor teachers, but that they have learnt to manipulate the system and put on a show for the DSA, only to return to their successful teaching as soon as they have departed from the examiner. Other excellent teachers refuse to play the game and so receive a lower grade, possibly imposed by someone who is not an expert in their field of work and who maybe has never had the experience of even being in practice as a driving instructor. The fact that we all know it happens, just shows what a farce it is. 'Looking forward' can only begin, when Check Tests are abolished.

If learners are unhappy with the training they are receiving, please do not necessarily blame your instructor, it may be the way they have been taught to instruct, or maybe they are struggling to make the best of the situation they find themselves in. Most ADIs would welcome CPD as long as it was relevant to their clients, but until the DSA thinks through the implications of its system, the emphasis of some of the instructor training may continue to be inappropriate and this will be passed on to the clients and lead to the failure of many otherwise capable students.

It seems obvious that the harder the test is made, the more the system will continue to fail, since the problems are linked with both the inappropriateness of the teaching and the testing. The Government suddenly seems to be appalled by the number of students who are still unable to read, but I am also appalled at the number of people who are disadvantaged by being unable to drive and then the increasing number of those experiencing the double whammy of being both unable to read or drive. Having worked on both teaching reading and driving, I believe the Government should be actively doing something constructive to address both the lack of reading and driving and there are answers to be found. At least there has been an attempt to improve reading, but nothing has been done for driving, except for the construction of more and more obstacles and increased discrimination amongst the disadvantaged and disabled.

****

In my teaching, I found that the stick never worked in the long term, because it was only used for the teacher's benefit and did not win hearts and minds, but let's consider the system of graduated licences I referred to earlier where the driver would undergo an assessment rather than a test and according to the level of expertise demonstrated receive a graded licence. I am not going into details, but because the basic level could be enhanced by further training, as well as it providing for the social needs of the elderly and infirmed, the public would be on the side of the Government and it would work. We don't have to do everything as we always have in the past. It does not have to be divisive and we can start again to develop a partnership to look at a different model.

v) **CONCLUSION**

A factor seriously affecting road safety is that the DSA, The Highways Agency, The DVLA, The Police, The Local Authorities and the Highway Code are all independent agencies singing from their own hymn sheets. I have first hand experience of this with regard to the markings on one of the most notoriously dangerous spiral roundabouts in my location, but if these agencies got together to coordinate their ideas into a cohesive policy instead of working contra to each other, then I am sure we could start to reduce the KSIs. Many people who drive on our roads will have their own ideas and these ideas should be taken into consideration by a public 'Think Tank', since the public are the ones who actually know the local problems and therefore know what they are talking about. At present they just see their young people dying on our roads every day and it irks when they are not listened to and have 'solutions' imposed from above which do not tackle the local issues, but politically make it appear as if something has been done.

I have only to refer to the problem of dangerous overtaking in my area. No lay-bys are provided for tired drivers; drivers who need to answer mobile phones; tractors to pull into; elderly tourists who don't want to drive at sixty and wish to give free passage to let the bunching cars overtake; learners who are inexperienced and may need to drive more slowly and compose themselves; drivers who need to read a map or need toilets; caravans who need to go more slowly, so we get the imposed solutions of occasional double white lines and dangerously sited speed limits which result in erratic overtaking. Like many concerned drivers I am appalled by the Government Departments who attempt to brush matters of life and death under the carpet by sending banal replies to serious concerns. It does amaze me that some of them get into these elevated positions because if I was marking their essays for GCSE course work, they would fail for having missed the point. These are just a smattering of my own ideas to show that we, the public, can think of new ways. To summarise the future of the driving instruction industry as I see it;

1. Coordinate the policies of Agencies involved in Road Safety:
2. Scrap Check Tests for experienced ADIs and develop relevant CPD:
3. Cap the PDI register and stop misleading advertising:
4. Raise the status of ADIs to driver educators and change their title from Instructors to Teachers:
5. Carefully select Potential 'Driving Teachers' before offering entry to the Register:
6. Provide ADIs with the skills to educate both children in schools and adults in the community about Road Safety, in addition to their regular role of teaching learners:
7. Introduce Graduated Licences with an incentive approach:
8. Move from the negative fail culture toward the positive success culture:
9. Actively change methods of teaching to reduce the dead spirits as well as the dead lives:
10. Get the public on side by providing believable accident statistics, stating the primary causes which are then broken down under the categories of heavy-commercial, private, motorbike, cyclist, pedestrian, illegal, unlicenced, overseas licenced, inexperienced, emergency services, and the effects of alcohol/drugs/medication.

****

The Driving Teachers would then be able to understand where and how to effectively target their educational efforts.

The Police would know where to target their preventative and correctional efforts, rather than being blamed after the event.

The Legislature would know where to target their laws and the effective level of penalties to set.

The Highways Agency would be encouraged to liaise with the other agencies to make effective engineering alterations.

The Road Safety Partnerships would be able to focus on issues acceptable to the public, rather than having to defend safety policies against the present public perception of hidden taxation.

The Care Services would know where to provide for the driving needs of those less fortunate than the majority.

The Public would at last be on-side, because they would understand what was happening and would appreciate the fairness of what they saw.

*These measures would effectively win the public Hearts and Minds and therefore create a successful and credible safety **Partnership.***

EPILOGUE

I hope this book has provided you with food for thought. My purpose for writing was not to profit financially, but to stimulate discussion in order to improve the lot of some of our learners and instructors. Please feel free to pass it on and even if its contents have not been your experience, others may find it is the answer to their difficulties. Please ask permission if you wish to reproduce any part of the publication. Further copies can be obtained via the information on my web site, which will also contain information about my next book,

DRIVING IS turning disability into ABILITY.

This will consider true examples of some of the people I have taught whose needs are not usually being met by the system normally practised. I hope it will help learners experiencing difficulties to understand they are not alone and also help instructors to be more aware of some of the problems encountered by those with Specific Needs. It covers a few who have had to decide that driving can no longer be appropriate for them and learners I have taught who have had to overcome these conditions:-
****

Abuse, Accident Trauma, Alzheimers - Dementia, Amputees, Arthritis, Aspergers - Autistic Spectrum Disorder, Bereavement, Body Dysmorphic Disorder, Cancer, Cardiac by- pass, Cerebral Palsy, Chronic Fatigue Syndrome (ME), Degenerative Disorders, Depression, Dyslexia, Dyspraxia, Educational/Emotional/Behavioural Difficulties, Genetic Disorders, Head Injuries, Joint Replacements, Language Disorders, Multiple Sclerosis, Multiple failures - confidence loss, Obsessive Compulsive Disorder, Parkinson's, Perceptual Problems, Phobias, Profoundly Deaf, Repetitive Strain Injury, Spina Bifida, Stress, Stroke etc.

&

The Agencies who seek my professional help: Advocacy, Car Dealerships, Disability Agencies, DVLA, Education Departments, Employment Services, GPs, Geriatricians, Hospital Consultants, Insurance-Legal Companies, Local Auth, Magistrates, Motability, Occupational Therapists, Physiotherapists, Police, Probation, Psychologists, Road Safety, Social Services etc.
****

I am often asked to recommend instructors who think differently and I believe we require a register of those who offer an alternative approach. I would appreciate hearing from any instructors who wish to retain their independence in developing suitable methods to meet the specific needs of their clients and would welcome any comments from learners or to hear of their personal experiences. Although I cannot guarantee you will get a written response, I will promise to read them and help in whatever way I can. **John Brown. (2008)**

systems2people@yahoo.co.uk
www.drivingincludesu.co.uk
Driving Is: Publications
6 BH21 2SR